THE RAPE OF THE POWERLESS
A Symposium at the Atlanta University Center

Authors: RALPH NADER
JULIAN BOND
IVAN ALLEN
MARK RUDD
SHIRLEY CHISHOLM
HARRY GOLDEN
WILLIAM OSBORNE

Editor: WILLIAM OSBORNE

GORDON AND BREACH, SCIENCE PUBLISHERS
NEW YORK • LONDON • PARIS

Editorial office for Great Britain:
    Gordon and Breach, Science Publishers Ltd.
    12 Bloomsbury Way
    London W.C. 1, England

Editorial office for France:
    Gordon and Breach
    7-9 rue Emile Dubois
    Paris 14e, France

TABLE OF CONTENTS

page

Introduction
William Osborne   1

Corporate Violence Against the Consumer
Ralph Nader   9

Feudal Politics and Black Serfdom
Julian Bond   41

The Urban System of Turmoil
Ivan Allen   73

Radical Students and Third World Revolution
Mark Rudd   95

The Black as a Colonized Man
Shirley Chisholm   133

Only in a New America
Harry Golden   159

Revolution and the Liberal Exploiter
William Osborne   185

INTRODUCTION

The evolving American multiversity increasingly pursues a dichotomous existence. Its context evidences enslavement as its content encourages liberation. Educational structures maintain fidelity toward established corporate form and ritual, but the transient constituencies within evangelize a revolutionary word. There would be pleasantness about this paradox, a more apparent creativity in the instability, if the relating of context and content were dialogical. Instead, the mutual suppositions prerequisite to conversation are obscured or absent, and the contemporary academic event suffers a malaise of unresolved and unreflective confrontation.

The American multiversity is now its own worst problem. Although idealistically interpreted as a monolith battling external forces of ignorance, its war is really within. The institution's context can tolerate some content of dissent but not the volatile dissolution of its own familiar structure. The institution's content is postured against external oppressions but also assumes the priority of overcoming oppressive internal forms and contexts. This house divided may stand, and, in a Marxist sense, the dialectical tension may be the harbinger of progressive new stages in the institution's history but, in the meanwhile, the mind-sets involved are increasingly rigid and the educational moment is acrimonious. "House nigger" and "field nigger" roles are identified and obediently played while neither total enslavement nor complete liberation is secured.

The dichotomy of context and content is demythologizing the American way of education. Pretensions of our academic past are scrutinized and increasingly exposed. The previous myths of value neutrality in subject matter, or egalitarianism of student bodies, or meaningful social mobility for graduates can no longer be promulgated unless, of course, with cynicism. The facile assumptions of those who determined the system's peculiar history are open now to empirical

1

refutation. Ezra Cornell claimed to have founded an institution in which any person could realize instruction in any study: the contemporary black revolt at Cornell, however, indicates that "any person" and "any study" have never been that university's *modus operandi*. Former President Coffman of the University of Minnesota boasted that state schools enhance the intellectual opportunities of every class or group, but state institutions particularly have been structured as vehicles through which an official, acceptable culture is imposed. Higher education in this country, as contrasted with Europe, has rationalized its being in terms of providing a levelling influence in the society, but the multiversity continues an earlier tradition of being the society's great stratifier, the institution which condemns or gives grace. And, this judgement as proffered is a major success determinant for an individual, a decision relegation him to succeeding enslavements or liberations.

The contexts of American higher education have never been insulated from the larger community; therefore, traditional charges of "ivory towerism" are not correct. The university of the past, and now the multiversity, has sanctioned and has been sanctioned by certain communities for certain symbiotic relationships. In early New England, the church needed the power base of a trained clergy and got it by establishing and controlling colleges. In early Virginia, the landed gentry needed to perpetuate classism in political life and did so by establishing and controlling other colleges. Following the Civil War, northern abolitionists needed to sanitize the black ethos, and southern whites needed to isolate it. Both established and controlled black colleges which nearly succeeded in their attempt at cultural genocide. Since the Second World War, universities have been criticized for their ostensive pledge of allegiance to the national government; in fact, the entangling alliances have been made through

government but with industrial and military collectivities. Far from insulating itself, American education has dynamically engaged in cronyism with those
community sectors which guaranteed an exploitable
relation. The *Realpolitik* of the multiversity is
not disengagement but exploitation.

The age of institutional innocence is over, and
it will not be resurrected through images which
were credible or at least palatable in our past.
The excesses of the church underwent sporadic refor-
mation until Luther, Erasmus and the sixteenth
century but, then, the authenticity of the system
itself was in doubt. Corruptions of political
democracies were periodically corrected until Marx,
Nietzsche and the later nineteenth century; there-
after, possibilities of representative government
were seriously questioned. The university has been
the last institutional sanctuary in our society in
which demagogy could take discriminate refuge but,
since the 1960's, the deceptions of this context
are revealed. The multiversity may now be interpreted as a corporation in the knowledge industry,
merchandizing a commodity which is sold to the
highest bidders. The market's demands are a priority,
and these may or may not have something to do with
less remunerative social needs. As a productive
element in a quasi-capitalist economy, this multiversity negotiates with and exercises responsibilities
toward its buying publics, and these postures often
contradict a responsiveness to a more total public.
Social organisms, such as the multiversity, cannot
be candidates for innocence: this is precluded
by that which motivates and is their *raison d'être*,
namely collective ego.

Existentially, of course, the academy's ego
is no longer truly "collective." The newer content
of all of the social sciences and even of such staid
disciplines as history and law acts as the conten-
tious agent within the context. The logic of a

corporation's sacrosanct role and status is treated
either as a threat or a comedy or both. Inside the
walls, there are economists who challenge the capitalist ethic, political scientists who are indebted to
a rhetoric of violence, sociologists who interpret
radical change as positive, and all find an impressive ideological target in the exploitive structures
of the multiversity. The urbane and revolutionary
presentations in the lecture hall do not guarantee
concommitant action, but they do suggest some tan-
talizing possibilities. Attempts to act out, to
actualize the theoretical commitments are increasingly
made as a charismatic student leadership, which has
internalized the content's values, appears. So, in
the 1960's, students at Columbia finally evidenced
interest in Harlem, that sprawling prototype of
ghettoes which the school in geographical and in
other ways has overlooked; students at Berkeley
endorsed some not-very-new linguistic symbols and,
depending on the analyst, created a "free" or "dirty"
speech movement; and students at more schools than
reluctant boards of governors would care to admit
rejected the concept that western studies are a
total curricular experience.

But, the dichotomy continues! Palliatives have
been offered within the context but not substantive
structural change: Princeton has younger trustees,
certain midwestern colleges have not renewed R.O.T.C.
contracts, and the University of Georgia provides
limited black studies. Further, alternatives are
available outside traditional contexts, but they
can hardly compete with the multiversity's expertise
and options: "free" universities and teach-ins are
organized, and independent research organizations,
some of which are also communes, have been established. The multiversity itself remains a fiefdom
which incorporates modest policy retreats as part
of its conspiracy to pacify the credulous and
maintain what is familiar. The content of the multiversity continues what is at times an insensitive,
antinomian dissent against most structures or what

is occasionally a more authentic vigilance against
the mediocre alliances of the present structures.
The turbulence of the dichotomy is not always con-
spicuous: there are interludes of campus tranquility.
But, as in any chronic state, a prognosis of health
based on the assumption that quietude means healing
is premature.

The moment most affected by the dichotomy is
the classroom where immediate structures of learning
are reminiscent of the mediaeval scholarium or the
nineteenth-century German lecture hall. As a micro-
cosm of the multiversity context, the classroom
offers motifs of enslavement and liberation which,
occasionally, are dramatized as faculty and students
experience offense from traditional roles the system
has assigned. If, in addition, the content of a
specific course encourages awareness of social
dilemmas, a class may evolve into a laboratory or
practicum where the abstractions of theory are
acted out. The result may be a mini-confrontation
over what forms are viable for an expression of a
subject area and, perhaps, either the modifications
of established routine or a continuing insistence
by students of redress for alleged classroom grievances.

The seminar lectures which follow in the
present volume had their genesis in this type of
dialogue and dialectic. A course entitled "Social
Conflicts" had been taught for years at the Atlanta
University Center. The academic source was usually
a textbook-toting professor and, increasingly, the
clientele were students with diminishing interest.
Particularly since the assassination of Martin
Luther King, Jr., however, a repetition of these
methodologies and responses was not tolerable.
As the largest and most important complex of black
educational institutions in the country, and with
a student body which was radically politicized by
the event of Dr. King's death, the Center experienced intense conflict over its academic identity.

Simplified, the issue was - and continues to be - whether a content of relevance to and probably revolution for the black community can be spoken and acted within a context which is largely financed by and maintains allegiance to representatives of white power establishments. One seminar could hardly answer a total institution's inquiry, but this seminar did assume an innovative posture which gave cognizance to the question and provided an alternative to questioners.

Three assumptions governed the new structure and content of the seminar. First, it was acknowledged that the most impressive teacher-informers in the life process of education are usually not official academicians within institutions of learning: they are specialists in action-knowledge who are able to analyze subjects out of a dimension of "grass-roots" involvement. Therefore, the seminar agreed to invite six authorities to participate whose experience in the area of conflict would not be related to professorial status and whose contribution would not be available, ordinarily, within the university. Second, it was agreed that those outside the confines of academic structures are one's academic peers as well as one's concern, and the seminar would provide a context in which the brother or other man on the block could be involved. As a result, communication was established between course members and the larger community including those who frequent "soul" bars and those who live in the communes of the hippie area of Atlanta. In every session but one, class enrollees were a very small minority of those who attended and dialogued. Third, a subject such as conflict must be entertained in a milieu which allows for its existential happening as well as its being theorized about, a site which can risk or even invite rough therapies. The Interdenominational Theological Center, the seminar's location, provided a freedom of verbal and physical interaction with leaders and session attenders pressing the flesh, holding by the lapels, and engaging in passionate if unorthodox linguistic expression.

The impact of this seminar's innovations on the Atlanta University Center may be partly conveyed through the edited pages which follow, but it is anticipated that this volume will prove particularly suggestive to other institutions throughout this nation, black or white, which are prepared to ask with some candor what the individual class should and might be doing. At present, there is no erasure of the multiversity's dichotomous existence but, during the interim, old contexts will be lived in and newer contents need to be spoken and acted out. It does not take a herniated imagination to visualize the likely failures of attempted relevance under these circumstances, but responsible actors must be willing to exist in such paradox and pursue what seem to be impossible possibilities.

WILLIAM OSBORNE
Professor of Social Ethics
Interdenominational Theological Center
Atlanta University Center

CORPORATE VIOLENCE AGAINST THE CONSUMER

Ralph Nader

My subject deals with consumer protection and corporate responsibility. I think the two are inextricably related to one another. They must be treated as one general problem, as different sides of the same coin. Otherwise, we will fritter away our legal resources and our moral energy on the syndrome aspects of these problems rather than going to the basic roots of them and trying to eradicate the preconditions of the consumer abuses in so many fields of our economy today.

First, let me define what I mean by "consumer protection." Basically it covers two areas: protection of the income dollar from erosion due to deceptive practices of shoddy workmanship goods and, secondly, protection against involuntary consumption, pollutants and acids. We are dealing not just with the abuses that tend to attach to a product willingly purchased; we are also dealing with the abuses that attach to the industrial processes making that product; for example, pollution of air, water and soil.

The first area is one which receives, of course, most attention in the urban-struck civil rights struggle, the constant conflicts that we see going on in the cities. This is the area dealing with the consumer's right to a legitimate product at a legitimate price.

One of the discoveries in this country in recent years is that the poor tend to pay more for their product and tend to get a shoddier product in return. Now,

this discovery was made many, many years after the conditions developed, much like the discovery that some
people in this country are hungry or suffer from severe
malnutrition.

In the city there has been a systematic channeling
of second rate goods, ranging from TV sets to food products into the slum areas. This, unfortunately, has
been done with the collaboration of some of the residents of the slum areas as the end product of the mar-
keting chain, such as an Indian reservation, for example.
Many of the problems stemming from Washington and the
surrounding areas involve or implicate some of the Indians on the reservations.

Perhaps there has been an excessive attention on
the civil rights issue in the cities by comparison with
what I would call the consumer rights, although they are
beginning gradually to overlap: they are simply a part
of the overall exploitive structure. But I became aware
of this distinction two years ago when I was involved
in what we may call the "unwholesome meat controversy"
in Washington which led to the strengthening of the
meat inspection rules.* This followed the disclosure of

---

* The passage of the Wholesome Meat Act, or any comparable bill with strength, had not been considered likely in the summer of 1967. The "agriculture reports" to
which Mr. Nader refers were a series of forgotten studies the Agriculture Department had made but had not used.
Nader obtained copies, passed the contents to the press,
encouraged a wide-spread campaign of letter writing to
the Congress, lectured, and wrote in such periodicals
as the NEW REPUBLIC. Although this campaign received
somewhat less publicity than his indictment of the Detroit auto industry, the political reversal it achieved
was of similar significance.

of agriculture reports showing atrociously unsanitary
conditions, the use of 4D animals for human consumption,
and the profligate use of either illegal or untested
additives such as coloring agents, preservatives, and
seasoning agents to mask the true condition of the meat
and make it palatable to the consumer.

I learned much of the volume of the 4D animals was
being channeled from livestock auctions in the midwest,
purchased by specialty buyers who deal in this type of
substandard meat and then channeled into the black slums
of Chicago. This was documented even to the point of
having pictures of the transportation of these animal
products; for example, carcasses being thrown in the
trunks of cars without any sanitary conditions that
should be used.

I tried to interest some leaders in the black community in Chicago and New York in this, and while they
were sympathetic, they were a bit disinterested. They
didn't consider this basically a very prime issue. I
am afraid that this is part of the overall lack of understanding, both in terms of the styles of the pressure which simply don't solicit much concern, and the
styles of modern environments which are assumed to be
almost entirely normal.

To give you a further illustration, we can, of
course, become quite indignant over rats in the slum
tenements. The tenants, especially, can become quite
indignant. In fact, the issue of rats has become a
focal point of what's wrong with the cities today. But
how many people have become excited over the fact that
slum residents are being exposed to a far greater degree
of pollutants than our suburbanites or people up on Park
Avenue? By "pollutants" I mean things like hydro-
carbons, carbon monoxide, nitrogen oxide that come from
the vehicle; the rubber, the particular matter that
spins off from the wearing of the rubber tires; the general dirty conditions of the city; the Consolidated

Edison plants that dump more and more of their pollutants in the deep core of the city, oftentimes in
the poorer areas; the basic pollution from industrial
activity.

In the area around Newark and Jersey City, which
is almost intolerable, people have been known almost to
pass out while they are driving their car on the Jersey
Turnpike. These, of course, all represent a different
type of violence, but they represent violence nevertheless. If anybody doubts the violence of these con-
taminants, there is a tremendous amount of technical,
biological and medical literature to rest these doubts
at ease.

The fact is that the nation, no matter which side
of the fence you are on, is caught up in an extremely
conventional and primitive context of violence-concern.
Violence-concern is really directed towards such things
as riots, stickups in the street and pushing and mob-
bing and, from the oppressed viewpoint, the kinds of
violence that proceed from visible starvation, the rav-
ages of deteriorated tenements, etcetera. It is quite
clear to me that the degree of violence stemming from
that area is relatively modest compared to the violence
that is inflicted on people, oftentimes without regard
for race, color or creed, by the processes of irrespon-
sible industrialism. Pollution in the air is one aspect; others are the almost total degradation of many
of our lakes and rivers which has a whiplash effect
back on our own health, on our drinking water; the number of people who are killed in vehicles on the highway;
the kinds of death and injury that proceed from flam-
mable fabrics in our homes; the kinds of violence that
obtain in hospitals, no less, with at least three people
every day being electrocuted in one hospital or another
in the land and something like 1,200 people being electrocuted with the cause of death termed, quote, "cardiac
arrest."

The comparisons, I think, need to be made and made quite clearly. When you have the kind of additives in our food products that are known to be carcinogenic,* are known to be adverse to human health in a number of ways, that's a kind of violence. It's violence when you attack the tissue structures of the human being just as if you attack his chin in some sort of more overt traumatic blow such as is subsumed under the problem of crime in the streets.

To give you a few illustrations, in the April 1968 disturbances there were 37 killed throughout the land. In the same week 43 people were incinerated and over a hundred badly burned in one little town in Richmond, Indiana when a gas pipeline, horribly maintained, full of leaks, blew up, almost destroying the central business district at that time. And yet that, of course, didn't make much headway in the press. In fact, it was buried in the press. To this day the town is virtually immobilized. Repairs have yet to be made. There is no law on the books, and there is such an anarchy, to use another term, in this field of gas pipeline safety that the Indiana Public Service Commission didn't even feel it necessary to investigate. In fact, it claimed that it wasn't authorized to investigate the explosion to see what the causes were.

---

* Carcinogenic chemicals are a group of about 500 compounds known to be capable of producing tumors in men and animals. All of them fall into a few chemical classes; some are carcinogenic only under particular conditions. The term "carcinogen," strictly defined, refers to malignant-tumor producers but is often used more broadly for compounds giving rise to benign tumors as well. The terms "tumourigen" and "oncoven" have been adopted by some writers and are nearly synonymous with "carcinogen."

To give you another comparison, if you take all the
riots in the last three years and throughout the nation,
you will see the total of 206 dead. That's less than
two days toll of violence on the highways -- less than
two days. If you want to take a comparison in property
damage, all the property damage in the same three-year
period in riots would not exceed $500 million. That's
one month's property damage to the vehicle on the highway.

Now, the point to be made is that as a society becomes more complex, more organized, more industrial, the
forms of violence also become more complex. Our psychological makeup, of course, allows us to react with
very quick indignation to the more primitive kinds of
violence, but we have not caught up to the period of
time, so to speak, whereby we can react similarly to the
violence of radioactive substances, carcinogenic substances, machine violence, whether it's in our plants,
foundries or on the highway. And I am afraid that in
the future it will continue to be that violence in the
cities will be more invisible, more complex and less
integrated in our framework of values and framework of
social action and concern.

The illustration on the radiation area a few months
ago caught some peoples' fancy, but then it quickly
passed away. It was learned that for decades technicians were exposing black people to a radiation level
during medical-dental x-rays of anywhere from one-
third to one-half more than white people. The folk
theory was that racial differences required higher levels
for black people. It's about the only thing that black
people get more of these days!

At any rate, the anthropologists that I consulted
indicated that in only one respect, density of bone
structure, could this ever have been the case. Therefore, an across-the-board increase of radiation exposure
was absurd. As one anthropologist said, "How black do

you have to be?" There is, of course, a great range of
variations. Furthermore, the reasoning for many of these
excessive exposures was due to totally mythical beliefs
such as the thickness of the skin, darkness of the skin,
et cetera.

Now, in the manual for x-ray technicians put out
by General Electric up to 1964 this was recommended.
In the training manual up to 1967, one of the prime
training manuals, the same thing was true. This has
finally been deleted and the problem has been recognized
at least by some of the professional societies, but
only after they denied repeatedly that this kind of
practice was going on.

Radiation is a form of violence. People are re-
ceiving by and large a far greater dose of radiation
during medical-dental x-rays than they need. In fact,
one estimate by the Oak Ridge National Laboratory indicates that about 90 percent of the dosage could be
eliminated and yet retain the amount necessary under a
suitable maintained machine which would take the picture more clearly.

Radiation, being a type of violence with an increasingly prevalent type of hazardous exposure as we
build more nuclear power plants and use radioactive
materials in all kinds of industrial and medical activities, is something to which we must accord a great deal
of respect. It is a type of violence that not only affects us in 10, 15 to 20 years, it affects our progeny
with impact on genetic structures. It is quite clear
that there has been very little consideration, at least
from the popular level, over just how adequately safeguarded the nuclear power plants are. In much of the
transportation of nuclear waste, radioactive waste, how
adequate are these safeguarded by the experts in Washington and elsewhere whose ability to compromise the public
safety tends to be higher than necessary, because they
want to promote the use of atomic energy?

The fact is that while we will guard Brinks' trucks, who are transporting a few million dollars in their armored cars, the transportation of radioactive waste and radioactive piles is done with the kind of lack of security and safeguards that are astonishing if not dismaying to many of the scientists that I have spoken with.

When we are dumping this radioactive waste is another problem. There are several depots in the country; we, of course, are throwing them off in the offshore areas in the ocean. But how long are these containers going to last? What happens when they begin to disintegrate? It has been disclosed that the government is transporting by rail nerve gas, enough nerve gas to kill a billion people. Anybody who knows how safe the railroads are and how up to date the equipment is might be a little concerned about this mode of transportation!

The area of auto safety is another one that has escaped public popular concern until very recently.*

---

* Mr. Nader's volume on auto safety, UNSAFE AT ANY SPEED: THE DESIGNED-IN DANGERS OF THE AMERICAN AUTOMOBILE (Grossman), was popularly received when published in 1965; actually, the book was a continuation of less-publicized auto technology research he had begun in the middle 1950's. The Harvard Law Record published his article "American Cars: Designed for Death" in 1958, which was followed by other periodical contributions and by an increasing number of testimonies to state legislative committees. By 1964, Nader considered local efforts somewhat irrelevant in this field and decided to attempt reform at the Washington level. Urbanologist and government official Daniel P. Moynihan arranged for him to work within the context of the Department of Labor, which eventuated in Nader's collaboration with Senator Abraham Ribicoff's committee and its hearings on highway safety. The National Traffic and Motor Vehicle Safety Act was passed in 1966, and

It's quite clear that, depending on how you design the
vehicle, you can build into it terrific potential for
violence when and if the cars go out of control and
crash.

For many years the whole philosophy of driving
safety was, "It's up to the driver." If the driver
fails, the car crashes. Cars don't animate themselves,
the drivers do. Of course there are several things
wrong with that analysis. First, it is grossly incom-
plete because the adequacy of the driver is very much a
function of the adequacy of the vehicle. If all drivers
were perfect perhaps there would be no crashes; if all
vehicles were perfect perhaps there would be no crashes
either. There would be essentially a device which would
activate the braking system automatically pending a collision. The question basically is where can we make the
most progress? By trying to deal almost exclusively
with the driver, 95 million of them in all kinds of contexts, or by dealing with a far more controllable sphere;
that is, the engineering, design and construction of the
vehicle? The latter would reduce the risk of accidents
in the first place by improving braking and handling et
cetera but also, and most importantly, it would reduce
the risk of death injuries in crashes if and when they
do occur. It would give people a second line of defense
so that if crashes do occur they need not lead to death
or injury.

If somebody is driving down the street and crashes
at 30 miles per hour into a tree, and the steering column impales him fatally, nobody asks anything other than,
"Well, was he drinking, or why was he careless at the
wheel?" Many of the so-called reckless driving crashes
are from falling asleep at the wheel and involve carbon
monoxide, as we were reminded when General Motors re-
called 4.9 million cars because of carbon monoxide leak-

----

editorials such as the Washington Post's claimed the
credit for legislation belonged to Mr. Nader.

age in the passenger compartment. You can't taste,
smell or see carbon monoxide, but it doesn't recipro-
cate that consideration for its victim.

The point that has to be made is that as we become
more and more an interactor or appendage of machines or
systems produced by the science of the engineers, the
amount of care that is taken in design of these machines
is critical to the level of violence that's going to
result from their use.

I think there is something basic we have to ask
ourselves again and again: why we do not get indignant
over this kind of violence? There are several reasons.
One is that much of the violence is a tradeup, an immediate benefit for deferred harm, such as radiation,
and what is in the future tends to be of less concern
than what is in the present.

The second reason is the mass brainwashing of the
public by our corporate brethren basically instilling
in many, many systematic and non-systematic ways a feeling among the people that we adjust to the machine, that
the machine is given and if something happens it is because we fail somehow to adjust to it.

Of course, the rational and far safer attitude is
to put a terrific pressure on the machine to adjust to
human beings, such as to redesign a steering column,
which could have been designed back in 1900, not to ram-
rod back as a spear into the driver during a collision.
The choice is between the human body adjusting to sharp
edges, weak doors and passenger compartments and all the
other hazards inside the car, or the car adjusting to
the human body's requirements during a crash. It is
quite apparent that the more efficient and humane way
is to make the machine adjust, to make that factory
adjust to the residents by not polluting the air; not
to have the residents around the factory simply to take
it as a cost of doing business on the part of the plant.

The consumer problem also involves the increasing

complexity of trying to keep up with the new kinds of
swindles that are perpetrated. One is the credit life
insurance matter. It's getting so you can hardly buy
a product, a consumer product, on time without having
to take out credit life insurance at a terrifically
high rate, a fantastically high rate in terms of the
premium that is being paid. Many of the companies,
were even going to the extent of including in the price
of the product the cost on the insurance policy without
letting you know that you were buying insurance. And
when you paid the cost of the product, you would be
taking out a policy: in other words you were being subjected to a forced sale. This is going on with many
automobile dealers. The point is, it is very, very
lucrative, tremendously lucrative, oftentimes 50 cents
on the dollar, 80 cents, and a dollar on the dollar
profit for that type of insurance. One can only bleak-
ly reject the type of merchandizing policies which in
effect instill or inject into the billing system these
kinds of hidden costs.

   Another problem is the moving of shoddy merchandise
into the poorer areas. In Washington, D.C., for example,
you pay much more for a particular product around 14th
and U, northwest, than you do on Connecticut Avenue, and
the product oftentimes is a reject.

   Now, when I mentioned this at a conference once an
economist stood up and said, "But there's one thing you
left out." And I said, "What?" And he said, "That the
residents at 14th and U could have gone over to Connecticut Avenue and purchased that set." It is about a mile
or so. This is the kind of explanation that fails to
take into account the hidden resistances to selling to
various customers in many stores today; it fails to take
into account the immobility of many people in the slum
areas; and it fails to take into account many other
subtle pressures which people on the wealthier side of
the fence simply cannot understand.

   Another area is the problem of law and order. This

is one which peculiarly amuses me as a member of the
legal profession. The legal profession never was concerned about law and order when it·came to the building
code enforcement. They taught students about collapsing corporations for 35 years, not about collapsing
tenements. They were never much concerned with the kind
of flagrant violations of institutions almost perfectly
efficient, a violation of the law as the cities began
to deteriorate. The cities deteriorated·almost in direct proportion to the violation of the laws which were
oftentimes quite well written but never enforced. This
abuse led to a whole system of bribery, payoffs and the
most profound corruption of the cities' processes.

The problem of the loan shark in the cities, fan-
tastic rates of interest, this too never concerned the
law schools until recently. The law schools were more
concerned with creditors' rights, not debtors' rights.
Even the courses were called "Creditors' Rights." They
weren't concerned with these laws, and I think it's a
reflection; this is the legacy which we are living with
now. It is something on the order of a half million
lawyers who came out of these law schools oriented and
trained to deal with the problems of the wealthy and
not only untrained to deal with the problems of the
poor but totally ignorant. There were many lawyers who
came out of Harvard Law School who never knew the slight-
est thing of what was going on in the cities except in
the Wall Street area, to which they went posthaste.*

----

* Mr. Nader once described Harvard Law School as a
"high-priced tool factory" because of its concern to
prepare lawyers to service banks and corporations. His
own educational era of the 1950's, sometimes judged
notoriously apathetic, was unresponsive to his early
attempts at Princeton University toward campus reform.

With the failure of the practitioners to engage in
this type of problem, you have a real domino situation.
The most important single factor in the rule of law in
this country is the lawyer, quite clearly, not the
courts, not the legislatures, not the agency. It's the
lawyer who initiates and takes the case, who defends it,
who prosecutes it, who knows how, in effect, to operate
and lubricate the legal system with a sense of justice.
And these lawyers are very, very much miseducated, poorly educated or basically trained to ignore the massive
problems of the many and concentrate on the problems of
the few.

One of the clearest contrasts here was a study of
estate planning or estate law. At Harvard Law School
we studied a mythical million dollar estate of a Mr.
Black. That's what we studied! When we got out of
that course we never had an inkling as to the probate
mess in this country which, of course, affects far, far
more people than the number of people affected by million dollar estates. Somehow, the wealthy can find a
way to take care of their problems, but the problems of
the probate courts and the problems of the small estate
were ignored.

Now, I think the recent trend in the law of the
establishment of neighborhood Legal Aid centers is
healthy in one respect but very limited. We shouldn't
have too much hope in it. What it does is to get some
of these young lawyers who have gone to law school into
the cities, rubs their faces in the kind of problems
which will stay with them for the rest of their lives;
whether or not they practice, they will at least be
aware of them. But it is a very inefficient allocation

Fellow students were not interested in challenging administrative power nor in defending what Nader thought
were student legal rights.

of legal manpower, in my judgment. We could have
300,000 lawyers in the neighborhood Legal Aid centers,
and we wouldn't have enough to represent the poor from
that angle of their problem.

Instead of representing 500 people against loan
sharks, it's a far more efficient strategy to apply
some of this legal talent to the insurance, finance and
banks from whom the loan sharks receive their financial
nourishment as it goes from the marble pillars down into the ghetto in the sequence of exploitation. This is
a far more efficient way. The same is true in many of
these other consumer abuses. They tend to proliferate
from the source, and if you deal with the front ranks
of the proliferation you need a great number of people
applying themselves, and you never get to the roots of
this problem.

And so we come back to a basic aspect of the problem, which is "corporate responsibility." The country
is organized in such a way that most of its foods and
services are processes of the corporate institution.
Unfortunately most of the mass indignation in this
country has been focused on government, whether it is
the Department of Agriculture or the local police chief
or sheriff. That is partly due to the fact that these
happen to be more visible. Corporate leaders are not
very visible at all.

To give you an illustration, for every 10 governors you can name in this country, I doubt whether you
can name one president or chairman of the top 40 corporations in the land. They are anonymous, deliberately. They don't go out to speak very much except to
their own trade groups. In fact, I have yet to locate
one single instance of a president or chairman of the
board in the top hundred corporations standing up before a university in a give-and-take exchange of ques-

tions, answers and address. There is a good reason why
this is not done, because the whole corporate structure
perpetrates its deleterious effects on society through
a very, very intricate process of insulation -- insulation of all other kinds of interactions.

It is an interesting comparison that while sena-
torial candidates, presidential candidates, guberna-
torial candidates go into the slum areas and go to the
cities and meet with the people, you don't see that
currently from corporate executives whose products and
processes have a far more direct and deadly impact on
these residents than these representatives who are going
up for election.

Southern California is a case in point. The heads
of auto companies have never gone to southern California, even though for 20 years the air in that area of
the country has been almost uninhabitable. The pollution
from the motor vehicles is such that 30 physicians a few
months ago declared publicly in a statement that anybody
who wants to care for his health should get out of Los
Angeles. That's how severe the pollution problem there
is, and it is almost exclusively from the motor vehicles.
They have cleaned up most of the other sources.

It seems to me that what was begun in the '30's by
way of attention to corporate power, but disappeared in
the '40's and '50's, should now be resurrected. We have
a concentration of economic power in this country which
is going to leave us with 200 corporations owning 75
percent of the manufacturing assets of the land in six
years. It's now up to about 65 percent. The merging
tie seems to be going along almost without stopping.
The government doesn't seem to be doing anything to
stop it. The fact is, we have a far greater capacity

to eliminate many of these problems, such as environmental pollutants and exploitation of the economic areas, than we are putting to use. Like many other countries, we have our problems; unlike many other countries we have terrific resources to do something about them.

Now, the question is how do we bridge this gap. I think it is time to meticulously begin to analyze the corporate structure to see, indeed, how much disclosure should occur about its products and processes; to see, what sort of sanction should be applied. I am continually amazed at how easy it is to escape the legal penalties of sanctions simply by wrapping a corporation around a particular individual. The gas pipeline explosion in Richmond is just one example, but we could cite many, many more. Buses going off the highway because of re-grooved, almost bald tires, time and time again, deaths and injuries. The maximum fine under the law if they prosecute a bus corporation, is $500.

On the other hand, eight months ago two teenagers stole 300 pounds of tobacco from a Maryland farmer. They were apprehended, it was their first offense, they returned the tobacco, and they were sentenced to three years in jail.

Basically, there is a terrific difference between individual behavior and corporate behavior and the results of both. The problem in the auto area is blatant. An individual driving his car down a highway negligently killing or injuring someone, can be subjected to a criminal offense charge and put in jail. But the auto companies, having deleted the criminal penalties from the Auto Safety Law, can wilfully, knowingly allow defective cars to go out on the highway, not delaying or recalling them at all, no matter how many people are injured or killed as the result, and there is no criminal penalty

evident. The maximum fine, for example, that General
Motors could be fined for such behavior is about
$400,000. That is equivalent to something on the or-
der of 13 minutes gross revenue from General Motors,
the company which takes in on the average, 24 hours a
day, 2.4 million dollars an hour. The whole process
of sanction has crumbled. It's no longer even what it
used to be when it comes to corporations.

You may remember the great electrical price fixing
conspiracy which broke in the early 1960's and finally,
under the Sherman Anti-Trust Act, several of the executives with GE and Westinghouse were sent to jail, all
for six-week terms which was the maximum. This was for
a criminal violation, engaging in wilfull price-fixing
which, in effect, cost the consumer well over a billion
and a half dollars. Now, what occurred was they were
fixing prices of electric generators, hiking the price
up, and the big buyers of the generators, such as municipal power systems, would pay much higher prices.
They would pass the cost down to the user, to the apart-
ments and homes in America.

The big customers had a right to sue General Electric and Westinghouse under the law for triple indemnity, but they didn't sue them in the sense of going
to court and trying the case; they settled out of court,
and the settlement was a $500 million settlement. But
just before the settlement General Electric and
Westinghouse decided, why should they pay all of that
$500 million? So, they persuaded the Treasury Depart-
ment to issue a ruling which indicated that such puni-
tive damage settlements as the result of criminal violations of the law could be deducted as ordinary and
necessary business expenses. And fully half of the
damages was hoisted onto the taxpayer's back.

This, incidentally, is the only type of socialism
that these corporations like -- that is, they like to
socialize their risks onto the public treasury and onto

the taxpayer. When it comes to any kind of socialism
other than that, they don't want it. But this kind of
socialism they have perfected in many, many ways as
anybody who tries to go through the legal maze in Washington would realize.

I would recommend far more attention be given to
equal protection of the law, so to speak, in this area.
I would suggest far more attention be given to how the
corporations are getting together and restraining innovation. For example, the restraint of innovation in
car propulsion systems is leading to this terrific pollution problem, allowing it to persevere. We don't
have to have cars that pollute the air; we can develop
cars with engines that don't pollute. Even steam engines, believe it or not, years ago solved most of such
problems. But they were never used. They don't sell
as well in terms of spare parts as the internal combus-
tion engine which begins tearing itself apart the minute it leaves the dealers' showrooms, affording the
large aftermarket for the auto industry.

The same is true of food distribution. To show
how it works in reverse -- not the restraint of innovation, but the application of innovation which is
really contrary to the public interest - the processing
of food occurs in such a way that the whole nutritional
value is stripped. The Department of Agriculture comes
out almost every year with the same old song saying,
"We have never had so much food; we have never had less
nutrition," and the well-dressed young boy in Scarsdale
sips on his Coca-Cola and chews his bag of potato chips.
Basically it is the kind of innovation which requires
long-term preservation of food from spoilage, putting
preservatives and all kinds of ingredients in food in
the laboratory. These have not been tested, and anybody who thinks that the Food and Drug Administration
has tested them is under an illusion. Food and Drug
is the first to admit that out of 500,000 chemicals
abounding in this land, they have a fairly good idea

of what 50,000 of them do to the human body. The rest
is like throwing dice up in the air. Products are made
to sell now and test later, such as the artificial
sweeteners which millions of people have been digesting,
many of them ordered not to increase their weight.
Suddenly out of the Food and Drug Administration, two
months ago, we learn some belated tests have shown
chromosome breakdowns as the result of the ingestion
of saccharins in drinks. The question, then, is how
can we allow the principal generic power in the land
to go so unscrutinized, to hide behind the secret of
the corporate facade?

Anybody who thinks government power is the chief
source of power in this country today is wholly mistaken. Government power is largely derived from the
way the economic patterns of the economy are organized.
The U.S. Department of Agriculture is a reflection of
the power structure in the farm and agricultural economy. Much of what goes for big government is due precisely to the needs of big business. In fact, big
business couldn't live without big government subsidizing
it, protecting it against competition, giving it large
six-scale contracts, allowing it all kinds of tax privileges, et cetera.

I think one illustration I can suggest to show you
just how exquisitely adaptable the corporate structure
is to all kinds of reforms and how necessary it is
every few years to constantly scrutinize these institutions is that of income tax. The corporate income
tax in many of these concentrated industries has become
little more than a sales tax. The corporate income tax
has become a cost of doing business to be figured in
before the product is sold, and the price of the product
reflects the tax.

In 1925, the corporate income tax was less than
half of what it is today. The profit rate of return
in terms of General Motors has not gone down; in fact

in so many years it has gone up. What has happened is
that the price of the car is reflective of the potential tax liability. So, last year General Motors made,
after taxes, about two billion dollars, before taxes,
four billion dollars; and in a ratio of return of investment that is at least as good as if not better
than any year that General Motors experienced prior to
World War II when tax rates were much, much lower.

You may recall the A&P when it was under the Anti-
Trust attack by the Justice Department screaming out
that it only made one cent on the dollar of sales. Of
course, that is an old technique to talk about return
on sales and not return on investment. In a situation
that accompanies the high cash flow velocity, one cent
return on sales isn't bad at all, particularly when you
consider what the investment is. But General Motors,
to give you a comparison, last year returned about 21
percent on sales before taxes and about 10.5 percent
after taxes; it was much higher on their investment,
ranging between 20 to 25 percent after taxes on their
investment.

I think it is time we discussed all the health
problems of the nation. We must ask ourselves this
question: why is it the most profitable corporations,
the real bullish stocks, are all in the health area --
the drug companies, the nursing homes? What kind of
society is this that gives the most needed services
into the hands of high-ranging corporations? One would
think it would be the reverse, for example, cigarettes,
candy, ice cream would be the highest profit, not the
most basic necessities of the population.

Let me conclude with these remarks. I want to
really emphasize again and again it is necessary to
subject corporations, individually and together, to
the kind of study to which we are now subjecting our
local government agencies and what have you. By this,
I mean even corporations that may not be in the top 40;
wherever companies are creating problems. There are,

for example, small chemical companies exposing their
workers to terrible occupational hazards. You may
know the big chemical companies by and large no longer
produce the most dangerous chemicals; for public relations reasons they have spun off these activities,
and little tiny suppliers now produce these and sell
their entire output to DuPont and Dow Chemical Company,
etcetera.

It is quite clear that students once in a while
should go to these areas and study these local problems, particularly around corporations, instead of
spending all their time in the libraries getting together a few sources for some critical matter or other
and then homogenizing it into a paper.*

I think it is very illuminating to go out to do
these interviews, to see how evidence is manipulated
or suppressed, to see what the students' impact is on
the process. The student will get an inkling as to
the power of the individual citizen who persists in a
line of inquiry on these institutions.

Now, because the student feels strongly about the
problems and tends to ask more and more questions, he
tends to have a more indelible educational experience.
We have an example of what happens to a region when that
does not exist, and I'm talking about Appalachia and the
presence of black lung disease in coal regions, the

---

* Educators increasingly support Mr. Nader's thesis
of extra-classroom involvement, some claiming in addition that academic sterility is a planned result by
professors who are inhibited by life "outside the walls."
One California State instructor has written of the student "as nigger," correlating the educational experience,
its disfranchisements and enforced irrelevancies, with
Southern black existence.

Coal miners breathing black dust over a period of years
and having their lungs strangled by this, in effect,
lethal disease. Europe discovered it in the '30's;
they developed a Workmen's Compensation; they did research for prevention.* But, in 1968 and '69 in the
United States only one state, Pennsylvania, gives the
miners Workmen's Compensation. There is virtually no
research done of the dust content of the mines. It's
one of the highest in the world, and nothing has been
done. When I asked what the University of West Virginia
had been doing about the problem, the answer was it had
been reflecting the economic power structure in its
reasoning, so it had been doing nothing. One wouldn't
expect Harvard to study black lung disease, but one
would expect the Universities of Kentucky or West Virginia to study it. But it was taboo; it was off
limits.

    The Law schools are even more at fault. One law
student came up to me and he said, "Do you know I just
looked through all the back issues of the West Virginia
Law Review and there isn't a single article on pneu-
monomelanosis and compensation?"† That's exactly it.

---

    *European writers have protested occupational dis-
eases of these types for three centuries; Blake, Lamb
and Dickens were concerned about malignancies of the
skin among chimney sweeps long before the American
"muckrakers'" journalism. In a volume published over
twenty-five years ago, Alice Hamilton expressed aston-
ishment at the "strange silence on (such) subjects in
American medical magazines and text books; I gained
the impression that here was a subject tainted with
socialism or with feminine sentimentality for the poor."
See EXPLORING THE DANGEROUS TRADES, Little, Brown and
Company, 1943.

    †Mr. Nader's reference is to the disease acquired
by inhaling coal or other dusts, whose particles may
be as small as one-half to five microns in diameter

When the educational process reflects the power align-
ments of its immediate environment, it virtually re-
signs from any impact that it could have on the contributions it could make to problems of all kinds.

I end with this suggestion, that such questions
be asked insistently in terms of corporate power. I
often wonder, for instance, what happened to the analysis of the '30's in terms of concentration on land-
owning power in this country and why there hasn't been
an adequate recognition of it in the '60's, particularly in regard to the corporation farms that are beginning to move in throughout the midwest and south-
west. These all, of course, have great implication
for a large part of our rural economy. Contrary to
most popular impressions, the greatest tyranny in this
country is not from Washington, it is not from New
York, it is the local tyranny. It is the most insist-
ent and the most efficient tyranny as far as the people
living in the locale are concerned. It's the company
town where the plantation areas have perfected the techniques to such a depressing extent; it's a concentration of these local tyrannies, I think that we need
to bring focus upon these before we decide what to do
about more generic umbrellas of oppression. Many times
the abuses from the U.S. Department of Agriculture are
nothing more, nothing less than an escalation of the
local tyrannies which, through the political process
leading to the Department of Agriculture, freeze an improvement of policy or prevents more public interest
action from taking place.

---

but, when retained in the lung, produce pathologic
changes. Nader is increasingly concerned about the
related disease byssinosis, now being termed "brown
lung," which is associated with the inhalation of cotton dust and which, he has said, afflicts an estimated
100,000 active and retired cotton mill workers. The
American Textile Manufacturers Institute, while claiming an aggressive interest in byssinosis and its cure,
has conceded that "medical investigations to date have
been sporadic and limited."

And so, contrary to these bogeys of federalism, creeping federalism and so on, the strings are still being pulled by the local communities. In area after area, it's at the local community level where the action has to be if we are going to have a more vital community responsible to state and federal governments.

DIALOGUE WITH RALPH NADER

QUESTIONER: You made a statement about radiation exposure and about manuals which recomment certain amounts, and so on. I have been practising dentistry for 17 years, and I have never in all this time seen any reference to color in relation to amounts of radiation. Did you mean a particular kind of radioactive treatment?

MR. NADER: No, these are the conventional medical-dental x-rays. I could tell you where you could write to get the evidence on this if you wish it. The Senate Commerce Committee in Washington has a large hearing volume with much of this information.

QUESTIONER: I thought you said it was part of the manual of training?

MR. NADER: Yes. It was in the General Electric training manual accompanying the x-ray machines up to 1964 and then the reference was dropped.

QUESTIONER: I imagine because I'm a black dentist they gave me the "other" manual!

MR. NADER: Incidentally, this was confirmed by the radiologic technicians in California who conducted a survey and found something like 80 percent of the respondents indicating that they did give greater dosages.

It was confirmed by the New York Department of Health, Education and Welfare.

QUESTIONER: I would like to ask, is there serious research being done on the problem of fraudulent advertising practices of private corporations regardless of their size? I ask this especially in regard to contests at filling stations and so on.

MR. NADER: Yes. This particular problem is now being investigated, finally, by the Federal Trade Commission in Washington. They had hearings recently, and dealers came in almost en masse opposing these games as being just a technique to enrich the oil companies and deplete dealers' own pockets. I think the days are numbered for these games. Probably you get rid of one game and then another one comes up. We just don't have adequate authority either at the federal or state level in these consumer protection organizations or agencies.

For example, one of the things needed badly is a preliminary injunction so that you don't have these things drag out for years; by that time the games will have outlived their usefulness and something else comes up. Or consider advertising, which is grossly deceptive. By the time the Federal Trade Commission gets around to it - it's a kind of a sleeping commission to begin with - the advertising is finished. And then they write in their conclusion, you know, where they tell Congress why they didn't do anything, and it is said, "Well, the advertising was suspended and therefore the problem is moot." Meantime, new advertising comes in, and it is a neverending scale. So we really need tougher laws at the state and federal levels, particularly injunctions to be brought.

QUESTIONER: Would you speak to the matter of auto warranty?

MR. NADER: Yes. Auto warranty, so to speak, is

hardly worth the name. It's the warranty given the
purchaser of a new car by the manufacturer against defects in workmanship and design - not all the car, just
certain exclusions here; the warranty was cut in half
in the last 24 months to 12 months and probably will be
cut further in the near future.

The basic problem of the warranty is that it is so
full of loopholes and so dependent on the integrity of
the dealer doing whatever he wants to do and whether he
feels he wants to do it. He doesn't get as much pay per
hour from the manufacturer as he does for working in
the non-warranty areas. The question is, what is it
worth? I get more complaints about car warranties than
any other category of complaints, by far.

So the recommendation, I think, that needs to be
accepted is to get rid of the warranty as it now stands
and simply declare across the board that any sellers of
new cars warrant for the life of the car against defects
in workmanship and design, period.

QUESTIONER: Mr. Nader, what about public opinion influ-
encing the creation of a Department of Consumer affairs?
I seem to see no results.

MR. NADER: That proposal has been made for a number of
years. I think it is gaining momentum. A hundred representatives in the House of Representatives will sign
the bill to create a Department of Consumer Affairs.
It's a reflection of a very interesting development over
the last 20 or 30 years: the government agencies which
are designed to protect the public tend to be captured
by the industry they are supposed to regulate - you
know, like the Interstate Commerce Commission, the truck-
ers and the trains and the Food and Drug Administration,
the drug companies and so on.

So, it was a recognition of the failure of the regu-
latory agencies to take into greater account public in-

terest issues, not just industries, which led to the
idea of "Well, let's have one department that deals
with nothing but consumers." There are administrative
hearings and so forth. Up come the lawyers from the
industries, and they represent their clients quite well.
And then on the other side nobody's there. Or, when
there is an official docket for a proposed rule-making,
for example the problem of how safe tires are going to
be, and the proposal is made by the agency and printed
in the Federal Register, comments are invited. In come
the congressmen, the tire industry, and what comes in
from the public? Once in a while you get a one-page
letter from some discontented tire owner who had his
tires blow on him at 4,000 miles. That doesn't carry
too much weight. In Washington you've got trade associations, corporate law firms, all kinds of companies
with offices, all kinds of agencies knowing who, where,
what's happening, getting preferential access before
the citizens know what is going on. And so the idea is
to get a department there staffed with lawyers, engineers, accountants and economists and getting them before
Federal Communications, getting them before the Food
and Drug Administration, et cetera. That's the idea
behind it.

QUESTIONER: I have heard a lot said about the injus-
tices of industrial society. Do you have further
suggestions of what could be done in particular industrial contexts?

MR. NADER: Let's focus on the corporation as a sort
of axis you have. First of all, the existing tools
aren't used. Workers have access to some of these. They
are inside the plant in their unions. The unions aren't
doing enough. They are not even doing enough about
their own in-plant safety for their workers. The United
Mine Workers leadership is now, you know, all "Executive
Suite" in Washington, hobnobbing with the coal executives. They have forgotten about the rank and file.
They just might have a revolt on their hands in West

Virginia. So one of the major access points is to wake
up and reform the unions. The dream of the '30's is
becoming the nightmare of the '60's as these union bu-
reaucrats just increase their salaries and their pen-
sions and forget about what they're there for in the
first place, about the rank and file.

        The second point of access is through shareholders.
Take a few of your major polluters in your area, major
steel companies, perhaps. One share will get you into
that shareholders meeting. From there, need I advise
you further?

        Thirdly, we have processes of lawyer's litigation.
Most people don't realize that for many, many years the
law has given them the right to sue corporations for
negligently designed products that lead to their injury.
In fact, to give you an idea of what the frontiers are
like, there is a plant that produced a deadly pollutant,
probably one of the most deadly pollutants abounding in
the country today, carcinogenic. A woman was living in
the area for 15 years, the fumes were all over her; she
was breathing them. She brought suit against the company, got an imaginative lawyer, and obtained a verdict
of $77,000. It's now being appealed.

        You see, there is no reason why neighborhood
citizen's groups cannot say, "We are sick and tired of
you perpetrating this kind of long-range violence on
ourselves and our children and our progeny, and we are
going to sue you for damages and an injunction to stop."
It's interesting in a sense that you get a quick injunction if there is a big pig sty smelling up the
neighborhood, but when a chemical plant is seething the
air around you with carcinogenic materials, it's very
difficult.

        What is difficult is not impossible, as you know.
A lot of things that were once considered impossible are
now facts. But you have to look at these kinds of access

routes.

Another thing would be to invite the president and chairman of the board to speak and ask questions at the university. If he says he hasn't got time, give him a five months lead time; give him a seven months lead time.

QUESTIONER: I would like to hear something about credit selling: for instance where furniture stores don't require you to have money, but the prices are high, the interest rates are high, and so on.

MR. NADER: Yes. You know there is a truth-in-lending bill which passed congress last year, and now it's being gutted by another law which would be proposed at the state level called the Uniform Consumer Credit Act, which was written heavily by financiers and bankers using law professor as fronts. The truth-in-lending law says that any state that passes a state law that is equivalent to the truth-in-lending law can be exempt from the federal law. This is the battleground. But basically, you see, there is just very little that can be done under the existing laws. You've got a large number of lawyers, neighborhood legal service lawyers, and a lot of times the furniture dealers will just relent because they know somebody can take them to court and drag them out and cost them money.

But I am for looking at this from the other side, from the sequence that leads to the furniture dealer and finally rooting him out that way.

QUESTIONER: I would like to ask a question about steam cars or electric cars coming on the market. What is really the problem? Do the big companies buy them off, or..

MR. NADER: They don't have to buy off; they just refuse

to accept. They so dominate automotive technology that
nobody around wants to tangle with them, and they will
only accept small inventions that don't have much re-
percussion. The problem is that they control the whole
development process right from production to the selling
of the cars. You can have a good car, but if you don't
have a dealer network you're going to have trouble getting it sold.

The problem became that you simply could not challenge the industry unless you wanted to spend about a
billion dollars and go into the business, and the big
companies outside, like General Electric, which is
working on electric cars, don't want to tangle. You
see, they sell computers. They sell products to the
automobile industry. They don't want to initiate a
major confrontation. It's too traumatic. G.M. could
then begin to move into their areas. It could be a
colossal struggle. And that's the problem; you don't
have real competition. They're all sticking out their
ears, tiptoeing all over the edges and trading off and
making sure; "Well, if you don't bother me about my car
I won't start telling the public that you are selling
light bulbs that last fewer hours than they did in
1930."

QUESTION: What is your evaluation of the American free
enterprise system? Is it viable in contemporary society?

MR. NADER: We don't have free enterprise. What makes
you think we have free enterprise? A competitive free
market system does not prevail here because of a great
many barriers - not just economic - that are built in.
For example, some of the barriers are purely transportation barriers. Did you ever try getting out of Watts?
It's very difficult. There is hardly any transportation
to go to many areas of Los Angeles, unless you have your
own car. So you've got these barriers that have been
built up. Why is there bad transportation in Watts?

Because we starve public mass transportation in this
country. Why? Because the auto industry has done
everything it could to make sure that automobile and
highway development take the primary claim on the public
treasury. It's like a vicious cycle: the fewer buses
the more need for cars; the more cars, the less customers for buses. The more pressure for highways, the
less pressure for mass transit. The highway lobbyist
is a well-known fixture in Washington. You don't get
much from mass transit.

Basically, business today is anti-competitive.
It believes in controlled enterprise, not free enterprise. It believes in a closed market system. It believes in price fixing, innovation restraint. It viol-
ates all the classical laws of economics. So don't let
them feed you with this lip service. The auto industry
gets up at the chamber of commerce and says, "We believe
in the free enterprise system." All right, one of the
requisites of the free enterprise system is to tell the
consumer about the product he's buying. Why? Because
then he can compare one product with another, one car
with another, and pick the one that he thinks is the
best, reward the best manufacturer, penalize the worst.

Try going by your dealer and asking him questions
about the quality of the car like brake-stopping dis-
tance, car performance handling. He will think you're
crazy.

QUESTIONER: That's not always what makes the car sell!

MR. NADER: Yes. That's another distortion, you see.
The distortion is that the control of the information
flow about a product is heavily in the hands of the
producer and therefore he can emphasize style, power,
interior decor in a car; the names - you know, whether
you like Barracuda or Cougar, all the kinds of flim-flam.
So, the people's attention is diverted to the psychological emotional attachments, and they never ask.

What in the world will we do with bumpers like that?
The bumpers on new cars don't even protect themselves.
And do you know what this means? This means - and this
is a very specific data - that every year the customers
pay the billion dollars in unnecessary auto repair costs
when cars crash together at five or six or seven miles
an hour, and there are no bumpers to protect the car from
property damage. That's a billion dollars of theft,
clear theft. You cannot say the auto industry doesn't
know what it's doing. You might say, "Well, they had
one off year," but year after year this increases the
sale of their parts and their fenders, which are very
highly profitable.

And so it's a distortion of the information flow.
In a perfectly competitive system, free market system,
the idealized form, the consumer has perfect knowledge.
Well, we're not asking for perfect knowledge. We are
just asking for some knowledge!

FEUDAL POLITICS AND BLACK SERFDOM

Julian Bond

What I want to do in this speech is to try to see
if we can help black people find ourselves in a great
many different ways, politically particularly, and to
attempt to go from a description of our condition to
some of the ways we have tried over the past few years
to improve our condition.

The first thing that strikes me about the condition
of the black people of the United States is that a great
many things in our lives have changed over the past several years, and among those things which have changed
most is our geographical position. We used to be, as
short a time as 30 or 40 years ago, a rural population.
But now, we are becoming and almost have become a completely urban population. That's the same kind of trend
that you can see in studying other groups in the country:
most of America is composed of urban rather than rural
people.

To cite a few examples, in the city of Washington,
our nation's capital, where we can't elect the dog
catcher much less a mayor, we are over 60 percent of the
population.*

---

* Capital cities, generally, enjoy a lower degree
of self-government than comparable urban areas in the
same countries. This is true in Paris, Buenos Aires,
Rio de Janeiro and, in terms of police administration,

41

In Richmond, Virginia; Knoxville, Tennessee; New Or-
leans, Louisiana; Jacksonville, Florida; Birmingham,
Alabama, we are over 40 percent of the population.
This city, Atlanta, Georgia; Gary, Indiana; Baltimore,
Maryland; St. Louis; Newark; Detroit; Trenton -- all of
those cities are going to have majority black populations by 1975.

In addition to our having undergone that kind of
change, we know in the past few years other sorts of
things have changed for us as well, and some of those
kinds of changes have been changes for the better. To
give an example, we can now eat in places we could
never eat in before. We can go to schools we never
could attend before. We can sit in the front of buses
that never used to stop for us before. There are more
of us holding elective offices in more parts of the
country than ever before, and there are more of us
making more money now than ever before. There are more
of us registered to vote and participating in politics
than ever before.**

_____

even London. The added irony of the Washington administrative process however is, as Mr. Bond implies, the
dramatic increase of disenfranchised black residents
who are politically controlled by Southern, white legislators through Congressional committees. Thus, the
problem of non-representation is compounded by the
possibility of ethnic imperialism.

** Representative Bond is one of eleven black members of the Georgia Legislature: there are two black
Senators in a total of fifty-four and nine black Representatives in the total of two hundred and five.
Black legislative influence, however, is considerable
in matters which relate to metropolitan Atlanta, since
the Atlanta delegation requires two-thirds approval on
local legislation, and seven of the twenty-four area
Representatives are black. These statistics do not

But for most of us, things have not gotten better.
They have tended over the past 30 years to get worse.
Let me substantiate that by reading to you from a speech
delivered several years ago by former President Lyndon
B. Johnson. President Johnson said in the speech at
Howard University in 1965 that in 1948 the eight percent
unemployment rate for Negro teenage boys was less than
that for whites. But for 1964 the rate for Negroes had
grown to 23 percent as against 13 percent for whites.
Between 1949 and 1959 the income of Negro men relative
to white men declined and dropped in every section of
the country. From 1952 to 1963 the median income of
Negro families as compared to white actually dropped
from 57 percent to 53 percent.

Since 1947 the number of white families living in
poverty has decreased 27 percent while the number of
non-white families living in poverty has decreased only
three percent. The infant mortality rate -- that is,
the rate at which children die the first year of their
lives -- in 1940 for black people was 70 percent greater
than for white people. In 1962 there had been some
change in the statistics: the figure was 90 percent
greater. I use President Johnson's figures. The rate
of unemployment for Negroes and whites in 1930 was
almost the same. For 1965, the rate for Negroes was
twice as high.

Now, when someone discusses those kinds of facts

---

reveal the growing national political influence of Bond,
whose constituency now includes diverse groups from the
old civil-rights movement, the peace movement and the
New Politics. John Lewis, the former S.N.C.C. chairman
and a Bond advisor, has said it is Bond who has the potential to emerge as a symbol which could represent the
varying factions as well as continue the leadership roles
formerly filled by Martin Luther King and Robert Kennedy.

and figures, he must be honest and candid and admit that
poverty is not the exclusive province of America's black
people. There are in this country a great many poor
white people as well; in fact, there are more poor white
people than there are black people, rich or poor. But
poor white people enjoy the rather dubious distinction
of knowing they are not poor because they are white but
rather are poor in spite of their whiteness. We have to
then assume that the racial problem in this country is
one both of race and class.

There are 3,500,000 Americans, both black and white,
who will on next Monday morning be looking for work they
will not find. No one knows how many million more have
given up looking for work and, therefore, are no longer
counted as being unemployed by the Department of Labor.

Unemployment in our neighborhoods runs between 30
and 50 percent as compared with about four percent for
the nation as a whole. There are 357,000 black men and
419,000 black women who are presently out of work.
Another 300 to 400 thousand are included in the hidden
jobless and aren't being counted as being unemployed.
Unemployment for black young people between the ages of
16 and 21 is six times as high as for white people of
the same age group.*

----

* The trends and their severity, which Mr. Bond
is emphasizing, correlate closely with recent private
and governmental studies such as the widely-dispersed
document issued by the Office of Policy Planning and
Research of the Labor Department and popularly known as
the "Moynihan Report". This research, whose official
title is THE NEGRO FAMILY: THE CASE FOR NATIONAL ACTION,
details the social pathologies which require correction
at the national governmental level and resolution
through one general strategy.

Now, if you were to examine the typical black
ghetto dweller, the person to whom all of those kinds
of statistics apply, this is what you would find. First,
if he is a young adult, there would be a better than 50
percent chance he would have dropped out of high school.
He not only would be unemployed but, by current standards, would be unemployable. He would have no saleable
skill. Neither of his parents would have gone beyond
the 8th grade. He entered school at six but, because
of overcrowding, would have attended half-day sessions.
During his six years in elementary school, he would
have attended four different schools.

The questions of the future ought to be "What has
been the past of this imaginary young man? What has
been his history and the history of his parents? What
sort of efforts were made by them or for them or on
their behalf to improve their condition?"

First, several things have been constant in the
United States for a great many years, and among those
things that have been constant has been racial violence.
Since 1917 this country has had continuous sporadic
periods of racial violence, and this violence has
always occurred during periods when the nation was at
war. Between 1917 and 1919, and 1943, and from 1965 into 1969, this has been true.*

_____

* The magnitude of such violent interactions has
been chronicled by John dos Passos in U.S.A., a three-
volume study of American social crises; by Arthur I.
Waskow in FROM RACE RIOT TO SIT-IN, 1919 AND THE 1960'S;
and especially by contemporary black writers such as
Nathan Wright who increasingly support the sociological
principles of "creative disorder" and "social disrup-
tion". In READY TO RIOT, Wright claims that "to live
without the possibility of violence is not to live at
all; for life at best is precarious", and he emphasizes

Since 1954 there have been various methods and
techniques directed at solving the problems that this
imaginary, statistical young man has. These methods
and techniques have included the sit-in demonstration,
the non-violent march, the pursuit of education as a
breaker of barriers, the use of violence as an induce-
ment to change, the challenging in the courts of segregation by law and the thrust for power through political
action.

Now, each one of these, very obviously, has its
own successes and its own failures. Legal action, as
an example, brought in 1954 a tremendous victory to
black people, a statement from the nation's highest
court that segregation in public schools was illegal.
But 14 years later in 1969, we discover there are more
black children attending all black schools north of the
Mason-Dixon Line than there were in 1954. Sit-in demonstrations, non-violent marches, have won the integrated lunch counter, the integrated toilet, the integrated bus station, the integrated movie theater and the
right to vote.

Each of these victories has had little meaning for
most black people who are economically unable to enjoy
them, and the last of these victories, the right to vote,
has yet to win real bread-and-butter victories for the
millions who are now voting for the first time. Education has often been suggested to black people as one
means of improving our condition as a mass, but I would
like to suggest that education as a means of improving
conditions dies every day that ghetto schools continue
to teach that "whiteness is rightness". Violence has

---

that overt expressions of violence are not as corrosive
or as pervasive as the "symbolic violence" continuously
inflicted upon the exploited by the exploiters
(p. 137 ff.).

been suggested as one sort of political technique to improve our condition, but I would like to suggest here
that violence has never had a real test in this country,
and the present national mood to me would suggest that
continued repression would follow long, hot summers.

In the past few years of this imaginary young man I
mentioned earlier, the country at large had begun to
change. In 1964, the community that this imaginary man
lived in was promised several things, among them that a
war on poverty would be fought and that poverty would
soon be eliminated. But just three short years later,
in 1967, the war against the Vietnamese people had
rendered that promise -- if it was ever meant -- completely useless. Between 1961 and 1964 this country
officially denounced violence and war as a means of
settling disputes between people or between countries,
but from 1965 to the present violence has been the official policy of the government of the United States in
settling her own disputes, and that belief, the belief
in violence, has seeped down into the police stations
and slums across the land.

In 1964, this imaginary young slum dweller I mentioned before thought that he might get a job, but
presently the only fulltime permanent job available to
him is being a soldier. War has angered the black community and has given birth to the belief that non-
violence is only a joke to be played on or played by
the black community.

When questions of violence come up one might imagine that black people in all the communities all over
the land ask ourselves these kinds of questions: whether
or not the status quo, the sorts of lies told to those
less fortunate than those of us here tonight, are not
just as violent as any Watts or Newark or Detroit? Is
it not violent to condemn to death twice the proportion
of black babies as white babies in the first year of
their lives? Is it not violent to send nearly twice the

proportion of black men as white men to Vietnam to fight
and die every year?

There are those people who believe that a non-
violent confrontation will force this government to turn
its attention homeward and toward a real solution of the
white problem in America. There are those who believe
that progress of a sort is being made and will be made,
and who believe, like Scarlet O'Hara, that tomorrow will
be another and perhaps a better day. And there are
those who are convinced nothing good will come tomorrow
unless the structure of today is changed by those who
willingly kill and die on the streets, either in frustration or in rage or in the faint hope that from destruction a newer and a better day will come.

Each of these, again, has its place. Non-violent
confrontations have their place. The English gave in
to Gandhi's repeated, massive non-violent demonstrations.
But one ought to remember the English were said to have
had a conscience, while this government is thought to
have none.*

If this is any indication of conscience, out of all
the members of the United States House of Representatives,

---

* Gandhi's interpretation of British responsibility
in India may be found in his volume, MY APPEAL TO THE
BRITISH, first published in India in 1942 with an American edition brought out by the John Day Company later
in the same year. The philosophy of "Satyagrapha" is
described by Gandhi in his work, NON-VIOLENT RESISTANCE.
Martin Luther King, Jr. correlated Gandhi's methodology
with the problem of conscience in America in several
volumes, notably STRIDE TOWARD FREEDOM. While Dr. King
continued his support of non-violence in the Gandhian
tradition, his later speeches revealed considerable
sensitivity to the complexities of power and, perhaps,
less expectation of responses of good conscience.

only 36 could be found who would support the recommen-
dations of the President's Committee on Civil Disorders.

If one looks for a solution to the problem that
faces us, a political solution particularly, one ought
to look at the places where the problem is concentrated.
Those places are called "ghettos," and they are described by Dr. Kenneth Clark as "social, political, educational and, above all, economic colonies." "Their in-
habitants are subject people," Dr. Clark says, "victims
of the greed, cruelty, insensitivity, guilt and fear of
their masters."* Using that kind of description, the
terms "colony" and "colonialized people" will then correctly describe the condition of those millions who tomorrow morning will be deserting the mechanized feudal
system of the south for the more highly mechanized and
more highly segregated ghettos of the north and west.

From those colonies, north and south, must come a
new kind of movement and new method. When one discusses new movements and new methods, one ought to think
back to the time of an earlier colony that existed before the United States and the method it took to free

---

* Dr. Clark's analysis is found in the book DARK
GHETTO: DILEMMAS OF SOCIAL POWER, where he distinguishes
between responses to the ghetto made by the colonizer
and the colonized. Privileged whites attempt non-recog-
nition of the ghetto dilemma; ghetto residents experience both the reality of colonization and, through mass
media, the life of the colonizer. According to Clark,
social revolt would be unlikely if the ghetto had no
knowledge of alternative life styles, but it is this
knowledge of the non-ghettoed world which leads to
hostility and despair, and which may eventuate into an
attempted destruction of the colonizer.

itself from oppression. That method was not peaceful
petition; it was not peaceful, non-violent demonstrations; that method was not requesting a redress of
grievances, that method was armed rebellion, insurrec-
tion, a seizure of property, death and destruction.
That was the American way of 1776. Now, if a new kind
of movement comes from the kind of movement that
existed in the early '60's, it has to be several things.
Among the things it must be is democratic, and that is
with a small "d." It must extend to every member of
the black community the opportunity to have a say in
who gets what from whom.

At this point, let me interrupt myself and say
something about what politics really is. A great many
people will tell you that politics is the art of the
possible, which means that some things are possible,
most things are not. Others will tell you that politics
is the art of compromise, which means that in order to
get what you want in politics, you have to compromise
on some other things. I have always felt that what politics really is is the art of seeing who gets how much
of what from whom. That's what is involved in it:
seeing who gets how much of what from whom. And we are
the "who" who haven't been getting how much of what from
you know who!

If we get our politics together we might have our
say in who gets what from whom, and so on. This politics has to decide that freedoms that are not enjoyed
in Watts or Sunflower County cannot be enjoyed in West-
chester County. It has to declare itself in the
interest of working people but not become the mistress
of organized labor. It would have to pay as much attention to a street light in a 50-foot alley as it does to
national legislation involving millions of people and
to international complications involving the future of
the world. It has to maintain a militarism and an ag-
gressiveness that will urge the respect of those whom
it seeks to lead.

If there are any kind of rules that are peculiar
to this new movement they would be these. (These rules,
by the way, are strange to some people but come from
rather moderate sources. One set comes from a former
editor of *Ebony* magazine, certainly not a revolutionary
journal, and the other comes from a former professor of
Atlanta University who now is at Duke University, which
is not a citadel of revolution!) These are the rules.
First, social, economic, educational, political and physical segregation and discrimination are quite evidently
very important for large numbers of white people. Secondly, appeals made to justice and fair play are out-
moded and useless when power, financial gain and prestige are at stake. Thirdly, positions of segregation
and discrimination will be adhered to until change is
forced through coercion from threats, through power or
through violence. Next, initiative for black political
and educational organization must come from within the
black community and must be sustained on a day-by-day
basis. Further, the geographical distribution of black
people makes black and white coalitions desirable but
only when based on racial self-interest and genuine
equality between the coalescent groups. Finally, and
most importantly, racial self-interest, race consciousness and racial solidarity must always be paramount in
the deeds and words of black people.* When self-

---

*   The "racial self-interest" of which Mr. Bond
speaks is interpreted by contemporary black authors,
such as Stokely Carmichael and Charles Hamilton, as
Black Power. Such interest or power rests on the premise that some methodology of this kind is prerequisite
to a viable black participation in a predominantly non-
black society. Carmichael and Hamilton state in BLACK
POWER: THE POLITICS OF LIBERATION IN AMERICA that "Before a group can enter the open society, it must first
close ranks. ... Traditionally, each new ethnic group
in this society has found the route ... through the

interest is forgotten, organized racism will continue
to dominate and frustrate the best organized political
actions of any group of black people and will leave
blacks powerless and defenseless.

This new kind of movement has to address itself to
several things: the solving of America's white problems, developing a new sophistication and consciousness
in the black and white communities, and making democracy safe for the world. This kind of movement will
succeed only if several things are done, and among
those things that must be done is to begin a rejection
of the kind of equality we are winning today. That
kind of equality is giving us an equal chance to be
poor and an equal chance to be unemployed, an equal
chance to drop out of school, and we have already won
without fighting for one bit a more than equal chance
to fight for someone else's freedom thousands of miles
from home. That kind of equality has to be suppressed
and replaced with an equality that provides full employment, guaranteed jobs or incomes and makes the
American nightmare become the American dream.

Only when we shall have gotten ourselves together,
only when we shall have decided who our enemies are and
where the battleground ought to be, only when we know
in our hearts we are right, and only when we demand our
worst sort be treated as well as America's best sort
will we begin to see whether this system and this
method can make a difference in our lives.

Having done all that, having put together that
kind of movement, having put in motion the kind of

"organization of its own institutions with which to represent its needs within the larger society." (p.44)
Thus, for Carmichael and Hamilton as well as for Bond,
race consciousness is not the continuation of racism but
the means of overcoming it.

forces that make up this sort of movement, one final and
further thing would be needed; and that would be something commencement speakers always speak of called "commitment." But in this instance it's the kind of commitment that would have done several things; the kind of
commitment that ought to have kept this section of the
country in the south in ferment from 1964 to the present
instead of our having seen the de-escalation in this
section of the country that we have seen; the kind of
commitment that might have kept the Chicago police force
busy for at least a day or so longer; the kind of commitment that might have insured a choice and not an echo
at the top of the ballot last November.

This commitment would require that each person interested in a movement like this keep in mind a rhe-
torical question posed by the late Langston Hughes, who
asked: "What happens to a dream deferred? Does it fes-
ter like a raisin in the sun or just explode?" If this
dream is deferred much longer then an explosion will
come, and in the words of an old song -- I'm sure this
audience knows this song that says: "God gave no other
rainbow sign, no more water, the fire next time."

DIALOGUE WITH JULIAN BOND

QUESTIONER: Mr. Bond, when you speak of the possibility
of the peaceful coalition in politics, how do you interpret the politics of Hamilton and Carmichael which
calls, I believe, for a whole new political party for
black people based on strength?

MR. BOND: I think you need that kind of party if you
believe that you will immediately have an effect on the
national scene. But, I think it's a mistake to think
that any group of political activists is going to have
an immediate effect on the national scene.

What I think would be better is to begin in a small way and begin to build up, because on that level it does not take a political party. For while I imagine it would be desirable to have one, and there are one or two examples of a black political party in the south, one in Alabama, I don't think it is absolutely necessary. Organized people don't need a party as much as they need, in my opinion, a notion of themselves and of what is important to them. Now, a party can help give them that, but they don't have to have a party to have that.

QUESTIONER: I want to ask if you think violence serves any positive purpose?

MR. BOND: I'll tell you this: if there had never been any violence in this country you wouldn't be speaking with an English accent right now. So, there is no question about the fact that violence can serve a positive purpose. It has done so in the past and will do so in the future.

QUESTIONER: Would you explain your position on substandard housing, particularly your bill before the Georgia House of Representatives, and would you tell us whether it has a chance of passing in such a legislative body?

MR. BOND: It has passed in the House and it's in the Senate now. What this bill concerns is this: suppose I'm a landlord, I own a piece of property that you live in, and the City declares that this piece of property is unfit for human habitation. Under my bill, if it becomes law, then you won't have to pay any rent. You will pay it to an escrow account established by a bank -- any bank. At the end of six months if I haven't brought the building up to code standards, you get to withdraw the rent and go elsewhere.

The trouble I find is that most people who are evicted from places that are demolished and declared

unfit is that their standard of living, their income,
is exactly the same, so they move into a house exactly
like that they just moved out of. The purpose of this
bill, or the effect of it, rather, would be that people
who do live in substandard housing might have a chance
to build up some money in the bank with which they can
move into a little better house.

As they say in the legislature, a simple bill does
one thing and one thing only: it's good for the little
man and all politicians like the little man.

QUESTIONER: Brother Bond, as you have seen the black
struggle thus far and have viewed the progress that it
has made, would you say that it is best for blacks to
incorporate themselves into a sinking and corrupt white
society or pull from it and work apart from this society
in an attempt to make things better for themselves? In
other words, should black folks join whitey or "split"
from whitey?

MR. BOND: I think that's not a decision that someone
such as myself can make for everybody. I like living
where I live, which is a black neighborhood surrounded
on four sides by black people. I'm not going to move.
I like the work I do in the legislature and have come
to the conclusion after not too much study that I am not
moving mountains in that body; but I like it, and I
hope the people I represent are grateful for the efforts
I make on their behalf.

So, I don't think it's something I can know for
you, or that ought to be dictated by any one person. I
think that's a matter for people to make up their minds
about by themselves and for themselves. I don't think
there is "a best way" for blacks. When I was I don't
know how old, people used to say to me, "All you all
need is this," and then they would name something. And
someone else would say, "No, that's not right; here's
what you all need. If only you all had this you would

be all right." Ever since, I have been suspicious of
people who say, "There is one thing we need and that is
this," because I don't think there's one thing we need.
I think there are many things we need. There are many
different things that suit many different ones of us.

I believe there is a popular song that says "There
are different strokes for different folks."

QUESTIONER: Mr. Bond, I have heard quite severe criticism leveled against Mr. James Farmer because he was
appointed to and accepted a position in Mr. Nixon's subcabinet. One criticism is, he was appointed because
the Republican party didn't have too much to do with the
blacks, and he is somewhat of a traitor to our position.
Those same persons would say that the black man in this
country isn't making any progress. Now, you like to
serve in your Georgia House, and I think you are there
because you care about your people -- I'm just assuming
that. I think Mr. Farmer's being in the subcabinet puts
him in a position to help his people. In fact, he is in
a department where most of his people will be greatly
affected.

Now, what do you have to say about these criti-
cisms?

MR. BOND: It would be easy for me to say I wouldn't do
what Mr. Farmer has done, but then I wasn't asked, and
I doubt if I will be! I have no criticism of him. I
mean I don't mind him going in. I'm not in a position
to say, "Don't do it, Jim," because I think he does believe he has an opportunity for service.

I think in this particular instance, however, he
is likely to be mistaken, because I think it is clear
Mr. Finch is not the decent man he is made out to be;
I think he may be one of the most dangerous men among
all the selectees in the Nixon cabinet. He is the man
who has given certain districts in the south 60

additional days in which to decide whether they will
obey a 14-year-old decision of the United States Supreme
Court.

So, I think Mr. Farmer may be mistaken in his belief that he can help black people in this way. At the
same time I may be mistaken, maybe, so I have no criticism.

QUESTIONER: Referring to the population shift of blacks
to larger cities, what effect do you think blacks will
have in the election of future mayors of Atlanta? How
would this relate to successes in Cleveland and Gary,
Indiana?

MR. BOND: An answer depends on several things; first, on
statistics. There is no increase in black registration
in Atlanta. We have 48 percent of the population, but
only 38 percent of the registered voters. Further, there
is also going to be a purge of the list this time,
coming just before the mayoralty election, which will
strike some several thousand black names and some white
names as well from the list. But that 38 percent, if it
goes as a unit, is likely to be the deciding vote, I
think, as it has been in past elections in this city.

I don't think there is going to be a black mayor
in this city. The two cities that have black mayors,
Cleveland and Gary, Indiana, have 50 percent or close
to 50 percent black registration, and that's what I
think it takes, because white people are not willing to
be mature enough to vote for a black person. We are,
apparently, because we have been doing it!

QUESTIONER: Mr. Bond, in reference to what you said
about a growing black population in Atlanta, you are
aware of a bill in the State legislature which is similar to bills before governing bodies in other states.
This particular bill states that by 1972 Atlanta will
become part of Fulton County or Atlanta and 10 other

municipalities in Fulton County will become one government. Your colleagues in the House of Representatives
say they are interested in giving the Atlanta city
government a broader tax base. This is their reason for
wanting to pass the bill. Do you feel this is the ac-
tual reason; or are they trying to keep Atlanta "lily
white?"

MR. BOND: I'm not able to look into other politicians'
minds. I will tell you this: I went to the Playboy
Club with Roy Harris, who, some of you know, publishes
a newspaper in Augusta, Georgia. He knows much more
about politics in this state than I do; he was George
Wallace's campaign manager in Georgia and Speaker of
the House for eight years before I was born. He told
me that "It's to keep you people down." And I think
Mr. Harris, who is older than I am, knows more about it,
and he's right!

QUESTIONER: There seems to be a period of oppression
going on over the country now, and at each stage of the
black advance towards equality of freedom, there seems
to be a stretching of the guard. I think the police
now have taken on the defense of white supremacy. There
seems to be no way out except violence. Are we headed
towards an enlarged racial conflict?

MR. BOND: I don't really think there is any way to predict. However, I think it is probable that that is
going to happen. I have no notion what the outcome will
be. I would suggest again however, that population figures would indicate we would be on the losing end.

     To go back to what you said earlier about the
police being defenders of white supremacy, that is really
unfortunate for us, in a way. It is unfortunate for us
because it makes us react against the police, who are
not responsible for themselves. For, if we see the
police as a single enemy, we are deluding ourselves. It
is not the individual, the policeman, who assigns himself to a particular block or who says to himself, "I'm

going to behave in a certain way," but someone superior
to him and in the chain of command someone superior to
that superior. I think we make a mistake to think the
police are the single enemy of ours.

QUESTIONER: Don't you think we should be like boy scouts
and "be prepared"?!

MR. BOND: Well, I think everybody should be prepared!

QUESTIONER: Ralph Nader pointed out that one of the crucial points of concentration affecting changes throughout the country would be to focus more attention than
presently exists on the corporations or on the corporate
structure. As you have talked you have mentioned new
politics. How would you address these new political
rules that you have so outlined to the concentrated
economic evil that exists in corporate structures?

MR. BOND: The problem is how these rules are applied to
power other than political power. I think they are adjustable to fit an economic as well as a political situation. I tried to apply them to politics as this is the
topic I was given to speak on and also the area in which
I feel the most competent. I do think the difficulty
is much greater when facing an economic force than a
political force. But, the same things apply when making
a political or an economic fight. Race consciousness
applies in the economic fight as it does in a political
fight. I think such rules are adjustable, then, to
economic situation.

QUESTIONER: Is the two-party system as it exists presently in the United States a viable means through which
black people can work towards achieving the goals that
we have?

MR. BOND: I don't want to attempt to be dodging your
question, but I think that the only way to answer it is
to try a general answer, and that is all I am prepared

to give. The answer is "No, that it is not a viable
means of structure through which we can work towards a
general solution of our problem. But I think the kind
of political apparatus that we need is one that is directly responsible to us and to us alone, and I think
the difficulty in building that is that some past attempts have come from the top down rather than from the
bottom up. My opinion is when they begin from the top
down, they are doomed to fail. They will not succeed.

When and if efforts are seriously begun in a variety of locations with a rather general purpose of weld-
ing together an association of black interests and political parties or a coalition with, say, Spanish American
and Mexican American interest parties, then I think one
could obtain a viable solution.

QUESTIONER: Mr. Bond, you have made some unfavorable
comments about the term "black capitalism," and you have
introduced something which you call "community socialism." Can you tell us more of what you mean by "community socialism" and how it will work?

MR. BOND: First, let me say something about "black
capitalism." This city of Atlanta is the center of
black capital development in the United States. Along
Hunter Street and Auburn Avenue there is concentrated a
great deal of wealth that is held largely in black
hands, and it is a fine achievement. These blacks have
enriched themselves and at the same time have provided
some employment for other people.

But capitalism as a political system quite honestly
would not solve the problems white people have, and
since we are largely an imitative group, why should we
believe that if it doesn't work for them it would work
for us? I just see no future in it solving the kind of
problems that we have. I am sure that an application
of black capitalism as I heard President Nixon describe
it would enrich and employ some black people. It would

build up additional entrepreneurship in the black community and would generally result in a higher standard
for some black people -- maybe many, but I tend to doubt
it.

My notion of community socialism is this: suppose
this building we are in now is a textile mill. It's in
the middle of the community, it's surrounded by black
people on all sides, and the people in the neighborhood
have jobs at this mill. Now, under black capitalism we
assume this factory would be owned by one or two entrepreneurs who would be assisted in their ownership through
loans and funds by private industry or the federal
government, and they would reap the profits from this
business and pay back the loans and then put the profits
in their pockets.

Under my system the factory would not be owned
singly or by one or two or three or four people but
would be owned by the community itself. The profit would
go back into the community and then some of the profit
someplace else to do something else. The notion would
be that the profit would not go into the pockets of two
or three people but, rather, would go into the broader
pockets of the whole community.

QUESTIONER: In light of what happened at the Democratic
Convention, what is your rapport or relationship with
the "Official Democrats of Georgia" at the present
time?

MR. BOND: I have no relationship with the official
Georgia Democratic Party. I ran for office as a Democrat; my name appears on the rolls as a Democratic member of the state legislature, so I get invited to go to
all of the party functions. I was invited to the Jef-
ferson-Jackson Day Dinner, I have two tickets. I returned them, not feeling that I could afford that meal.
And so I have almost no relationship at all; just never
met the party chairman, just don't know them.

QUESTIONER: In regard to your community socialism, how
would this differ from our current system where we have
stockholders in large corporations who also are supposed to reap some benefits?

MR. BOND: The difference is, I can buy a little stock
in General Motors, but I am never going to get as rich
as Charlie Wilson, who used to be president. He's not
going to give me any of the money my stock has helped
him get as president, and the majority stockholders of
General Motors are not going to share their stock with
me.

    Under my scheme stock would be sold only to bona
fide residents of the community -- that is, if you
lived in Sandy Springs (a wealthy white suburb of Atlanta) you couldn't buy any. If you lived here and
moved to Sandy Springs you would have to sell it back
to the corporation or back to someone else who lived
in the community. You could buy as many shares as you
wanted, but you would only vote one share.

    This would be the difference: the money would stay
here, circulate here, and no one would take it out of
the community.

QUESTIONER: What I can't understand is if you have this
community set up in such a way that all the proceeds or
dividends would be returned therein, how would you confront the problem of human behavior and the striving to
get ahead? Would you take that into consideration?

MR. BOND: In the first place this factory -- assuming
again this is a textile factory -- would be run by a
manager as all textile factories are. He would want to
get ahead, and he would want to please his employees,
who would be the community corporation that would own
his business. His employees, as a community corporation
would want him to get ahead because they would want to

increase the profits that would come back into the community to provide jobs. The motive for getting ahead
would still be there. However, this wouldn't be a gain
towards a simple acquisition of individual wealth but
towards an acquisition of wealth and improving life as a
whole in the total community.

QUESTIONER: In Soviet Socialism, where they supposedly
took the wealth that belonged to the state and distrib-
uted it, after a while "elites" arose. You know that
if a man achieves an elite status you have a similar
situation, a financial class over here. Are you taking
for granted that everybody in your system will have
wealth?

MR. BOND: No, I don't take it for granted at all. I
take it for granted that you will be able to control the
evil impulses of some men and channel them into creative
possibilities for the good of others.

Take what has been happening in China as an example.
You had the creation of the elites in China, you had a
revolution within the revolution, and a young man now
in jail in Argentina has written a book about that revolution within a revolution. I think what happened in
China, some of the things that he wrote about, suggest
that that kind of struggle is constant, that your revolution is achieved, the old order is upset, a new order is imposed, and the time may come when the new order will have to be upset and a new one imposed on it.
I think revolution is a continual process.

QUESTIONER: Representative Bond, I am going to ask a
question that I know is going to be the most ticklish
question of the night. I am not trying to put you on
the spot as such, because I realize you are only the
speaker. When you begin to talk about certain subjects
concerning the black people, I think that there is a
question of security. I have been noticing the gentle-
man here who is recording this, and I notice that he is

not of our race. Other folks are here who are NOT of
our race. I have noticed a pattern that started with
Nat Turner: every time the black folks move politically
we are infiltrated. Now, I said I was going to raise
the most ticklish question of the night, and that is
can there be black consciousness or race consciousness
with an open-door, everybody-welcome policy?

MR. BOND: I don't think there can from the very beginning, but I think there can be once such consciousness
is achieved. I think I have achieved it, so their presence doesn't disturb me.

     I think it is necessary on a great many occasions
for us to be completely by ourselves in our own meetings
where there is no one there but us. But I don't think
that is a rule that has to be applied to every context.

QUESTIONER: What is the right of the majority when the
minority protests?

MR. BOND: The right of the majority is to protect the
minority and insure its right to protest.

QUESTIONER: You spoke of solving the white problem. I
wish you could give me a definition of this problem.

MR. BOND: The white problem in America is the problem
that has caused us to suffer as we have. We don't have
a problem; we have many problems. But, the major problem is the white problem. We could solve one of our
problems and still be faced with this other major white
problem. So we don't have to solve any one of our problems; we have to solve the white problem, which is the
racism that has pervaded this country since. it was
founded. When that is solved all the attendant problems that we have will be solved, will disappear like
magic, almost.

QUESTIONER: Mr. Bond, what do you think of the students

who have asked in many of the colleges that we have all
black courses and all black dormitories? Would you comment on that?

MR. BOND: I have been to one college where that request
was granted, Cornell University in Ithaca, New York.
The black girls wanted a black house they could live in,
where they could be with people who play the same kind
of music and enjoy the same kind of music they did, enjoy the same kind of food they did and share the same
kinds of problems they had. So they made the request
of the school, and I think they had some difficulty but
the school granted it. I think the school acted pro-
perly.

One thing that bothers me about the present demand
for black history courses is I don't believe every
American university can or ought to offer complete, all-
inclusive courses in black history. I think the result
is likely to be that most of them would be very poor,
and I had rather see schools like Atlanta University or
Howard or Fisk or another collection of black colleges
become expert in, say, one black history, one black
African history, one black American history and so on.
I think these colleges have got to find their own
speciality and become the best in that rather than thinking every American university, white or black, is going
to be the best in offering all of these courses. I
think that just demeans the whole thing. There have
only been a hundred black Ph.D.'s in history graduated
in this country. Who is going to teach all of these
courses? The ones who are teaching at Morehouse are
going to get a big offer from Harvard and they will go
there, and then what will the poor Morehouse students
do? And so on.

QUESTIONER: I want to make a statement, and you can react to it. I don't know how many read it in the paper,
but Secretary of Health, Education and Welfare Finch has
ordered the University of Wisconsin to desegregate its

Afro-American, black dormitories. This not only happened at the University of Wisconsin; he has ordered
all major universities that have Afro-American studies
programs and black student unions and buildings and
dormitories to desegregate.

MR. BOND: I would guess if they are supported by federal funds then they ought to be. I don't think you
can have a double standard and say that the University
of Mississippi ought to integrate its law school and
then say another school someplace else ought to seg-
regate some of its facilities. I don't think you can
have a double standard.

But I do think certain schools can find ways they
can provide kinds of separate facilities. It's done.
You have off the campus of Morehouse a small, one-
storey house; it's there for all the students, but it's
primarily for the Episcopalians. I have never seen any
Roman Catholic students there. At some of the schools
I have been, they have a place for Roman Catholics; I
have never heard of a Baptist getting in there, and they
have houses or homes for Jews. I imagine some large
universities may have them for Buddhists.

So, I think there are ways that some universities
can do what has been done without running into the kind
of prohibition that's involved with the acceptance of
federal funds.

QUESTIONER: Brother Bond, this problem is not so pressing, seemingly, in colleges as it is in high schools
but I wanted to get your opinion. A large number of
people, in view of the desegregation of the schools,
find that when black kids move out of black schools into
white schools, there is a problem of going into the
white band and joining the white basketball team and the
white football team and this sort of thing. These activities may be good for building character in young
folks yet as one black young lady said to me, she is

not in the band because, well, she noticed whites don't
have soul! Thus the blacks dropped all instruments,
they dropped all athletics, etc. It is still important,
you see, to have separation, since people do things because of their own interests and in their own ways.

Now, what do you think about this?

MR. BOND: I know of an instance that has been reported
in the papers about a young black boy at Tennessee, I
think, who was put out of the band because he refused
to play "Dixie," and that may be what this young lady
meant by their not having soul. But I would suggest
that not all black people have soul either. There is
a very well-known country and western singer who is a
big hit in Atlanta, one of the most popular western and
country singers to come to Atlanta, Charlie Pride, and
he's black and draws them in down there at the O.K.
Corral or wherever it is. I don't happen to think he's
very soul, myself.

I wouldn't know what to suggest to a young person who is in that circumstance. Lew Alcindor has
little or no trouble, but I guess he's an exception.

QUESTIONER: A great number of the student government
officials are concerned about how the expansion of the
Atlanta University Center and its building projects
would affect your district and the people who have
always lived in it.

MR. BOND: No one is more concerned about that than I am!

The effect of this would be several things. It
would take the homes of a great many people who have
worked a great many years to purchase them. Now, the
school has made offers to some people, I understand, to
buy the land. Some of them have accepted and some of
them have rejected, and no one seems to know for sure
exactly what the status of this development plan is. It

is a frightening prospect, however, to hear the people
in the neighborhood say that they have no notion of
whether they ought to improve their homes, build
porches, fix up the steps, whether they should let them
go or whether they should be prepared to move, whether
they should stay or what they should do.

This is a pattern which has been set already by
Columbia in New York City, which is doing it in Harlem;
by Temple and Penn in Philadelphia doing it in South
Philly; it's something that most large urban schools and
universities and colleges are having to deal with, and
the people in the neighborhoods hope that the institutions will deal with it in a much better way. Present
methods suggest some sort of shortsightedness.

QUESTIONER: Inasmuch as the university stands for free
examination of knowledge, do you think that it is time
the university addresses itself to a universal body of
knowledge instead of the traditional body of western
knowledge?

MR. BOND: The western kind as opposed to what?

QUESTIONER: In western countries, we have addressed ourselves to knowledge in the western sense. However, the
university is supposed to be a center of learning where-
in you can confront a universal type of knowledge which
prepares students for the world instead of preparing
them for, shall we say, America or Europe or the western countries?

MR. BOND: I disagree with that for this reason: I think
people ought to be prepared for the world, but I think
some people are going to be more specialized, and some
people are going to want to be prepared for this part
of the world. I don't think the schools ought to try
to generalize too much in their peculiar history.

Schools ought to place a greater emphasis on

African studies. They ought not to be interested in the
history of Scandinavia as much as they should be
interested in the history of Africa. So I prefer to see
them make a concentration on that rather than try to
present the universal scope of knowledge.

I think if someone wanted to study the history of
Scandinavia he could go to the University of Denmark!

QUESTIONER: An increasing number of black ministers are
entering politics. From your experience in politics,
do you think this is a wise move?

MR. BOND: When I first ran for office a minister ran
against me. He was defeated. In this last campaign a
very well-known and popular minister ran for a seat,
which is the second time, and he was defeated. I don't
know if that means ministers are bound to be defeated
when they enter politics, or whether members of their
churches said what members of churches are likely to
say, that they have quit preaching and "gone to med-
dling" and they do not want their ministers involved in
anything besides the affairs of their church. It may
be that such people have what may be considered old-
fashioned ideas for the role of the minister, or the
ministers have too progressive an idea for their con-
gregations.

But I don't think it makes any difference what a
man's profession is if he goes into politics. It helps
to be a lawyer, because most of the other people in
politics are lawyers, and it makes it easier to understand if you are a lawyer; but it is not necessary.

QUESTIONER: Mr. Bond, you have been mentioned frequently as a possible contender for the office of mayor
of Atlanta, and you have quite frequently shunned that
idea. Nevertheless, I'm interested in knowing what you
consider to be the major issues in the mayoralty campaign of such a metropolis.

MR. BOND: The major issue in such a mayoralty campaign is going to be annexation. Another issue is likely to be property taxes, which will mean a great deal to large numbers of property owners of this city. Another issue is going to be race; obviously, it will be a primary concern. I don't know whether it will be largely a question of education in the schools and the racial complications of that aspect or whether it is going to be racial segregation in housing.

QUESTIONER: In view of the integration in public schools and many Negro students going to schools that have baseball and football teams named "Rebels," and in view of the fact we have in Georgia a state flag that looks like the Confederate flag, there are two questions I want to ask: one, do you think we are going to go back to the original Georgia flag and get rid of the Confederate-looking outfit; and, two, will some of these high schools tend to change the name of their football teams from "Rebels" to something else and omit the playing of "Dixie"?

MR. BOND: A lot of the schools have. In Florida, I understand, some schools have quit playing "Dixie," and some of the professional teams in Atlanta have stopped playing "Dixie" at their games.

The flag, I think, is going to be changed. Georgia has had its present flag only since 1955, and it's quite obviously a reaction to the Supreme Court decision. I am fairly positive that the state is going to go back to the old flag, and that the Confederate flag will be an object of history as it ought to be.

I think these schools in time are going to drop those names. They would be offended, for instance, if Washington High (a black school) were to name its football team "Vietcong."

QUESTIONER: I understand that a number of whites who voted

for Kennedy in '60 switched over to Wallace in '68.
Now, do you have any idea why this would be?

MR. BOND: It's true that in Lake County, Indiana, where
Gary is, Robert Kennedy carried in 1968 the same pre-
cincts that Wallace carried in 1964 when Wallace ran as
a Democrat. It also has been claimed that a lot of
people, poor white people particularly, said after the
convention that since Eugene McCarthy did not become the
nominee they would vote for George Wallace.

I think that is so. I can imagine someone who is
poor and white seeing -- and particularly in George
Wallace and Robert Kennedy -- much the same kind of man,
for different reasons. Both were small men, for one
thing; both were combative men and aggressive men,
against different forces but both very aggressive. I
would think to certain kinds of persons that is very ap-
pealing regardless of the nature of their political beliefs.

Some may question whether in fact George Wallace
fought as hard for what he said he believed in as he
did or whether Robert Kennedy did as well. There is no
question, I think, that they had the image of fighters:
Robert Kennedy began by fighting the evil Lyndon Johnson; George Wallace by fighting the whole evil federal
structure which wanted to impose its will on the "good-
hearted people" of the state of Alabama; Eugene Mc-
Carthy was the lonely figure who struck out by himself,
without any help from the Kennedys, against Lyndon Johnson.

Each one of them, I think, had the image in the
minds of large numbers of people in the population as
fighters; as a single, solitary, lonely, struggling
underdog. It's odd people could think of Kennedy that
way in spite of his great wealth, but I believe a great
many people did. Many people, I imagine, said to themselves -- even though they were poor, and neither George

Wallace nor Robert Kennedy nor Eugene McCarthy were
exactly poor -- "That guy is just like me. He's fighting the bosses, and I'm fighting them in my trade union;
I'm fighting them on my job; I'm fighting them on my
block; I'm fighting them in city hall. He's just like
me and I'm going to support him."

THE URBAN SYSTEM OF TURMOIL

Ivan Allen

I am interested in an opportunity to discuss urban life from the "nitty gritty", from the center of activity which is City Hall; for, City Hall is where the confrontations of the nation have occurred in urban America in the past ten years. I have no great background of philosophical thinking, but I have been exposed during these ten years to trying to find pragmatic answers to the problems of the day as an elected official in the largest and probably most progressive city in the South.* Contrary to

---

*Atlanta, often referred to as the "New York of the South," shares more social and cultural similarities with other major urban centers in the nation than with its own, more immediate geographical region. A large number of non-Southerners has moved to the metro-Atlanta area, whose population is the first in the South to exceed one million and whose rate of population growth is among the highest in the nation, nearly forty percent during the past ten years. The city is the transportation, communications, finance, and educational center of the Southeast, and nearly every industry of national scope has branch head-quarters in its area. At the time when Birmingham, Alabama and other regional cities used police dogs to intimidate civil rights demonstrators, Atlanta was promoting its image of a "city too busy to hate", electing Ivan Allen over Lester Maddox in a Mayor's race and, in 1968, giving Maynard Jackson, a black lawyer, a majority of its votes in his attempt to un-seat Herman Talmadge as Senator from Georgia.

most people who talk about these problems, I have
been actively confronted by both sides of the issues
and have had to look for very workable urban solutions. I'll talk about what the problems are as I
see them, what they have been, and what some of the
solutions should be.

    I came into the Mayor's office partly because I
had a program for the city. But this did not gain me
the office as much as the fact that I had been greatly exposed to the early beginnings of the civil
rights movement in the South. I was one of three
people who had attempted to solve Atlanta's first
major problem of voluntary compliance which was known
in those days as the variety and chain stores issue.*

----

    *Ivan Allen, Jr. was first elected Mayor of
Atlanta in 1961 with a power base built on a coalition
of votes from blacks and upper socio-economic classes
of whites. His winning margin of three to two over
(present Georgia Governor) Maddox was possible with a
nearly-even split in white votes plus support by 98
or 99% of the black community. However, Allen's influence in urban affairs, as he notes, predated this
election and originated out of his prominence in the
business community. Such a relationship between
economic and political powers, so common to the
American metropolis, is described in Floyd Hunter's
study of Atlanta as follows: "In the normal course
of events, the actions of the private citizen, at
least on a policy-making level of power, are almost
indistinguishable from those of formally designated
officials. The dual relationship between government
and economic operations tends to blur into one
process" See Hunter's COMMUNITY POWER STRUCTURE,
"Regional City", (Chapel Hill: University of North
Carolina Press), 1953. For further discussion of
Atlanta as a prototype of the urban power context,
see Kent Jennings' COMMUNITY INFLUENTIALS: THE
ELITES OF ATLANTA (The Free Press of Glencoe), 1964.

To someone 58 years old, which I am, and looking back over the past ten years, I can see vast changes that have occurred not only in the field of civil rights but in the general progress of the cities. But, I can see as well the horrible dilemmas that we are still in. In the international sphere, these include especially the foreign war to which four Presidents and eight Congresses have not found the answer; a war which is not supported by young people today although it was the idealism of previous youth that put America into the position of trying to defend the rights of men all over the world.

In the domestic sphere, however, the greatest problem for the urban centers of America, particularly those east of the Mississippi River although not exclusively, has been the racial problem. We have seen state governments entirely ignore this. In fact, I am not sure but that state governments have quietly attempted to increase the flow of rural people, who have been 80% Negro, into urban centers in order to relieve the states of pressure. Whatever has been the background of this, it can almost be stated as a fact that state and county governments have ignored this migration of people; that the national government has recognized it and tried to deal with it (I am not saying to what degree of success), but that the solutions have had to be sought in the cities of the nation.*

---

*The swift migration of rural blacks to Atlanta and other major urban centers in the nation has been documented by Vivian Henderson, President of Clark College within the Atlanta University Center and chairman of the Georgia Advisory Committee to the U.S. Commission on Civil Rights. According to Henderson, in 1920 there were more than 920,000 black farm operators in the South; today there are less than 180,000. This decline of 80% is a rate of decline 67% higher than that of white farm operators.

I have seen Atlanta in this past nine-year period
go through the throes of change. One-half of the
white population of Atlanta that dominated the city in
the late 50's and early 60's was vigorously opposed to
civil rights and verbalized their opposition loudly.

I have seen that change to where we have been
able to open Atlanta up on a fuller scale. This has
been accomplished through the five basic phases of the
rights movement that Congress has dealt with; school
desegregation in '54; the Civil Rights Act of '64
which included Public Accommodations and Employment;
the Civil Rights Act of '66 which included Voting;
and the Civil Rights Act of '68 following Martin
Luther King's death which was Public Accommodations.
In Atlanta, we have seen the transition successfully
carried out 100% in public accommodations; a great
improvement in the field of employment; a complete
success in the field of registration and voting rights;
no determination at the present time in the field of
open housing; and efforts made but not successfully
in the desegregation of the local public school system.

So, the effort has been made at a national level
to cooperate with certain local levels in which there
has been success in three of the five major fields.
And, Atlanta as a particular city has been generally
successful, although in one phase the results are not
yet known, and in the school problem attempts have not
been totally successful.

In raw figures, the black population of the rural
South has decreased from 6.7 million in 1920 to 4.7
million in 1960. Further, the rural farm black has a
median family income of one-third that of whites in
the South; 83% of black rural housing units are substandard as compared to 28% substandard housing among
whites. Dr. Henderson's conclusion is that migration
remains inevitable so long as the rural Southern
black does participate in the nation's affluence.

The racial issue today has gone to an entirely different position. We are now confronted with a violent spirit of reactionism in the country. There can't be any question about that! There is a very definite polarization of attitudes. This was easily seen by the Commission on Civil Disorders in their recent report.* That Report has been solemnly adhered to by most of the larger cities in the nation, but some of its suggestions have become political footballs. And, concurrently, this has brought about very strong feelings of dissatisfaction among many people.

What has happened in the cities as we have gone through the throes of this most important issue is all types of side effects which cities have had to face up to in providing equal opportunity for all their citizens. Let me put it this way: fifteen years ago, city governments had much the same attitude that I attribute to state governments today; they looked on society as two separate groups of white and black, and there's no question but that the white and the affluent received a degree of services

---

*The use of the word "polarization meets with some resistance by younger, black political leaders in the Atlanta area. Although most agree that separation is the social fact of this time, they reject implications that the fact is new, or necessarily increasing, or should not in some ways increase. When asked by the ATLANTA CONSTITUTION whether a further splitting of the races could be averted, Julian Bond was quoted as replying, "It's only white people I hear say avoid polarization. I think they say it because they think we're not already polarized. I think we are." Ivan Allen's present thesis acknowledges this past polarization, and his reference to a "violent spirit of reactionism in the country" and to the description by the Commission on Civil Disorders appears to implicate the white community in particular.

in the city that the Negro citizen did not. These inequities are changing very rapidly at the present
time although each city is at a different degree of
progress in correcting old deficiencies of the past.

In Atlanta, efforts to lay a foundation to
correct these deficiencies have had to come about
through the enactment and the utilization of major
federal programs. I don't think Atlanta as a city
could have tried to provide equal status of government
for all people had we not had federal guidelines that
insisted that these programs be carried out in an absolutely fair and impartial basis. There are three or
four hundred such programs, but basically they revolve
around the concept of low-income housing, whereby pro-
vision is made for people who in the past lived in de-
plorable conditions, were not accorded an opportunity
and who, by virtue of their inexperience coming out of
rural areas, found themselves locked up in complex
urban situations without the capabilities to cope.
They moved into the cities or they grew up in the
cities with hope and, yet, opportunities to exercise
their hope simply weren't there.

Utilizing possibilities of improvement through
low-income housing has not been an easy job for the
cities. You meet with the most bitter resistance concerning the location of such facilities as well as
the feeling by a large part of the white community
that the programs are unnecessary. Right now, 12 out
of every 100 people in Atlanta are living in low
income housing. This is somewhere close to sixty
thousand people in the city who are qualifying for
low-income housing. You can see the magnitude of it!
Atlanta operates about 12,000 units of low-income
housing now, and this has been stepped up rapidly
with additional units being constructed.

A second phase of and improvement upon low-income housing is the utilization of what we call "urban renewal".* This includes relocating vast numbers of people in slum areas to the periphery of the city and then rebuilding the older areas. Obviously, when you go into any major rebuilding program of the type and magnitude of urban renewal projects, you create some wrongs.

I certainly would not represent this phase as perfect. But, when you look at the general overall good that has come out of it, the tremendous improvement in the areas, the transposition of people into better living conditions, which can be proved, the virtue of urban renewal can be seen.

We are now entering into a third phase which again, is dependent upon a national, federal program and which is called "Model Cities." Here, as before, we are going a step further than we have gone. We are taking a major portion of the city of Atlanta and rehabilitating it: three thousand odd acres with about 60,000 people in it, 70% black, 30% white; six different neighbourhoods, two predominantly white, four predominantly Negro neighborhoods; an area which, fifty years ago, was the best residential section in the city but which has steadily deteriorated because of neglect by local government.

---

*The construction of low-income housing began comparatively early in metropolitan Atlanta with projects initiated in the early years of the first Roosevelt administration. However, urban renewal, as described by Mayor Allen, was not developed until well after the Second World War. The reasons were similar to those found in other major cities: one, state laws that prohibited resale to private enterprise of land purchased by the government and, two, considerable diffidence by important real-estate corporations.

In the old style of things, this area was turned
over to the Negro community as it spread out in the
city.* We're going in there, however, to try to re-
habilitate both its physical and its personal aspects.

This is an entirely new field for government in
the magnitude in which we are doing it. We are
attempting to set up all the educational values on an
entirely new scale, to make the educational facilities in this particular area superior to the balance
of the area of the city; to involve all of the social
agencies that hold some hope for improving the lot of
people; to improve the transportation facilities; to
rebuild the sewer system; to repave the streets; to
put in new lightning; to provide loans to rehabili-
tate every home where a person's income is under a
certain amount; otherwise, to run the whole gamut of
social experiences that the cities and the federal
government had been through in the last thirty years.
This is a terrific experience which could not possibly
be 100% effective because no program of social reform
this broad and this new could be on its first go-round.
And, there will have to be a great number of changes
made in it as we learn by experience which aspects can
be effective in carrying out these improvements.

There are dozens of other programs but, basically,
all have been created at a national level and provided
to the urban centers as a means of solving problems
that have come about with this vast migration of poor
people from rural areas. It is no problem to establish
and prove that my general approach is accurate.

---

*The changing ethnic composition of Atlanta, within
its city limits, may be correlated with that of Detroit,
Washington, and other major urbanized areas. In 1960,
62% of the city population was white, 38% black; by
1967, 55% was white, 45% black. Although there are no
accurate figures for the present year and month, black
citizens will consitute a majority in Atlanta if, indeed, they do not already.

You can take the pattern of growth and development
of urban areas in the past twenty years and find that
a substantial part of the established citenzry has
left the cities. The new mobility of the American
people has accentuated the process whereby older
sections of established cities have been turned over
to the immigration of rural people. And these are
people who have suffered the failure of an educational system, the lack of job opportunities, and of
health facilities·, rural people with no previous
civil rights whatsoever.

The cities, then, are caught up today in what is
almost a "system of turmoil": they try to provide
adequate facilities while operating under terribly
restricting charters granted by rural legislatures.*
Atlanta as a city could make a great deal more progress in coping with these problems had it the right
to determine its own destiny in the field of raising

---

* The dichotomy between the needs of cities and
the political controls exercised over them by rurally-
orientated state legislatures is reviewed at some
length by Jane Jacobs in THE ECONOMY OF CITIES. She
acknowledges that legislature power at the state
level, while an anachronism presently, reflected an
accurate distribution of power at the time apportion-
ments were originally made. Her claim, however, is
similar to Allen's insistence that turmoil results
when needs increasingly center about areas and groups
which, historically, have not been major decision-
makers. Jacobs affirms quite positively the inevitability of change, saying "economic development,
no matter when or where it occurs, is profoundly sub-
versive of the status quo". Thus, the economic productivity of urban areas will, itself, be the
catalyst in a re-distribution of socio-political
power between cities and states. See THE ECONOMY OF
CITIES (Random House: New York), 1969, pages 245 ff.

money and in making expenditures to effect the necessary
corrections. What actually happens is that the better-
known methods of taxing and raising money with equitable
methods are not provided in urban centers by the state
legislatures. A city like Atlanta, dominated by a rural
legislature, has not been given the right of a sales tax,
a payroll tax, an income tax, or any of the normal means
of raising substantial sums of money. We are still tied
to the old ad valorem method of the property tax as the
basic source of income. Therefore, we are restricted
from sources of income which are absolutely needed. And,
regardless of whatever respect and consideration is
given to the American dollar, we don't have any other
vehicle for making changes. This rural dominance is
creating a tremendous problem for every American city
today.

The fourth crisis that I would mention is transportation. The automobile is engulfing American cities.
We exercise no control over it and can't possibly provide for the rate of increase of vehicles. No school
would operate without some control over the number of
students involved in it. If you suddenly, tomorrow,
doubled the number of students in this institution, you
couldn't cope with the increase. Yet, this is what
the American city is confronted with today in the un-
limited number of automobiles pouring into it each day
from the periphery, plus the normal yearly growth which
is increasing at eight or ten percent. We have used up
the old established street patterns of the city, they
are completely saturated, and there are no basic funds
available for that which is the most expensive of all,
changing street patterns.

So, what I am saying in a very personal way is
that the American city, as exemplified by Atlanta and
as I have seen it through experience over the past ten
years, has these problems: the race problem, the rebuilding problem including the various methods I mentioned, the problem of finance, and the problem of

transportation. All of these are coming about at a
time when there are vast social changes of every con-
ceivable nature in our overall system.

The American democratic system however has provided broad ranges for such change and improvement.
This is evidenced as you trace the pattern of the last
one-hundred years: the abolition of slavery, the right
of the working man to collective bargaining, the abolition of child labor, the right of woman suffrage, the
social reforms of the thirties, the civil rights bills
of the 60's. The system itself is capable of change
for betterment. The problem we are confronted with
today is the rapidity of change in the 50's and 60's.
Alfred Whitehead said that major changes in a good
society are often the things that come closest to destroying it. He meant that the human being doesn't have
the capability of making the adjustment as fast as the
change can be made. This is one of the throes that we
are confronted with today.

Out of such urban crises, however, is going to
come a full citizenship for all American people which,
so far as the Negro has been concerned, has taken 105
years to accomplish. You are going to see better
representation at legislative levels all over the
country as a result of the one-man, one-vote rule. You
are going to see additional demands for reform as
better-educated young people move into positions of
responsibility. (Your generation certainly has indicated that it shares a concern in all of these fields.)
Eliminating the last vestiges of racial discrimination,
providing for more intelligent application of legislative principles in government, better administration
of these legislative principles, some way to control
the transportation problem, the solution of urban
financial problems, all of these things are evident
to me as I look toward the urban future. And most of

these will come about in a reasonable length of time as
the application of the one-man, one-vote rule takes
over and old rural legislators are pretty well swept
out of the picture.*

There will be what you would call a "renaissance
of the cities," which is the place where Americans are
going to live during the next hundred years. Right now,
we know that Atlanta is going to have two million people
in the metropolitan area by 1980, and three million
people, 3/8 of the population of the whole state, in the
year 2000. This growth of the urban community will continue, although sometimes I wonder, God knows, why everyone wants to live in cities! We are going through the
throes of change, but this change is part of the renaissance of the urban centers of America.

I've disclosed my own thinking on urban life, and I
would like to open this to questioning and attempt to
clarify any of the statements I have made.

---

* Mayor Allen contends that unless state legislatures throughout the nation dramatically change their
attitudes toward urban areas, political power at state
levels will be drastically curbed, and the vacuum will
be filled quickly by their federal and urban competitors.
Some state political leaders, such as Jesse Unruh of
California, concur. At the Citizens Conference on State
Legislatures in Atlanta, Unruh said, "For many years
now, our state legislatures have suffered decline of
status, dignity or independence... (they) have a low
regard for themselves and are poorly regarded by the
citizenry. A governmental body finding itself in this
depressed condition is no match for its formal partners
in government, the administration and the courts.
Neither is it a match for its informal partners in the
government process, the press and organized special
interests."

DIALOGUE WITH IVAN ALLEN

QUESTIONER: Mr. Mayor, Governor Lestor Maddox said that
you sabotaged his tax program! I wish you would clarify
this.

MAYOR ALLEN: You could't have asked me a nicer question!
In the first place, mayors ordinarily do not have great
influence over state legislatures. In the second, my
thinking is compatible with the thinking of urban-orien-
tated legislators.

     In the last session of the Georgia legislature,
there were vigorous efforts made to provide some income
for cities. Urban legislators, the Georgia Municipal
Association, urban governments in the state all backed a
bill which would have provided for an increase of one
cent in the sales tax and would have put most of this
money back into urban centers. Out of the one hundred
million dollars of the tax bill, the Atlanta area would
have paid about thirty-two million dollars and would
have gotten back somewhere between twenty-two and twenty-
five million. This was not absolutely fair; this imposed some burden on the city to help support the rural
areas of the state; but, we recognize we have to do that
to some extent. Then Governor Maddox proposed that the
Atlanta area be taxed the same amount, 32 million
dollars, and receive only 11 to 13 million dollars. It
doesn't take much arithmetic to figure out why people
paying the bill objected to that rate of interest!
I publicly state that I was opposed to that type of tax-
ation for the "benefit" of the cities when it would give
us back approximately a third of what we paid. We recognize that we are the wealthiest area, but we can't carry
the whole burden; that's all there is to it! We've
been financing rural counties in this state for a long
time, and we cannot continue to do that when the problems are in the cities today. The problems are no longer
in rural counties which are shrinking in population.
Their problems have decreased and ours are increasing.

QUESTIONER: In the local Model Cities Program, are
blacks a serious part of the decision-making?

MAYOR ALLEN: The Director of the Program in this area
is an outstanding young Negro citizen who came up
through the City Planning.Department; his staff is
over 50% Negro. The present requirements are that he
has to certify on any new personnel hired. He must
verify that there is no person in the area qualified to
fill a particular job before it can be hired from outside. I expect that we will continue to see local
Negro governmental talent in this program which is
dominated by Negro leadership.

QUESTIONER: What is your interpretation of "law and
order"? How does this relate to "crime"?

MAYOR ALLEN: These issues are about as misunderstood
as any can be. Questions of law and order, in my own
mind, break down into several different segments.
I would say that public officials are confronted with
maintaining law and order in terms of an orderly
society in the streets or in the schools and colleges
and, when asked to, the churches. This question of
law and order, however, is entirely separate from the
question of crime. I think that properly-run urban
communities with the right leadership can maintain
what I call law and order in the segments that I have
just mentioned. But, local officials and national
leadership today obviously do not understand the
tremendous increase in crime. We think that we have a
limited understanding of the conditions of crime in
Atlanta: we feel most of it comes out of the deprived
areas, and we are trying to correct the conditions in
these areas. This is the great emphasis of this city,
but this is not a program that's going to be effective
in six months. It takes years of education and job
opportunities and housing to alleviate deprivation.

We don't understand what is causing the present

tremendous increase in crime. The police force alone
is not going to correct it. There is no longer an
inhibitory fear of the police that there once was. We
don't understand why there is also so much nationally-
organized crime. Some say that's a national problem
and the national people say it is a local problem, and
the truth is that we are not correcting it at either
level. So, my conclusion to you would be that, as
Mayor of this city, I can maintain law and order, but
I do not know how to prevent the increase in what I
call violent crime that is going on at the present
time.

QUESTIONER: How does Atlanta stand nationally today
in rate of unemployment?

MAYOR ALLEN: Atlanta has done an excellent job in
widening employment opportunities and in eliminating
discriminatory practices. Our condition at the
present time is that we have, factually, the lowest
rate of unemployment of any of the national cities.
At the present, it's at two percent of the working
force which is about 60% of the national average. We
have had excellent response from employers in providing additional job opportunities. Our major problem is the totally unskilled, unqualified worker who
has no background to really meet job requirements.
I would say that 90% of the unemployment in Atlanta
today is unskilled, unqualified Negro women. That's
basically where all of our unemployment is. The
amount of job opportunities however is almost un-
limited.

QUESTIONER: Would you, as a previous office-holder,
endorse future candidates for the office of Mayor?

MAYOR ALLEN: No, I would not unless it reached a
point where I felt that there was a totally unqualified person about to be elected. I don't think that
I should intervene in a normal election and probably

would not make any personal commitment.

QUESTIONER: Have churches been able to provide leadership or help in areas of urban change?

MAYOR ALLEN: I would say that, in general, the
churches missed the boat in the Civil Rights Crusade,
if that's the right terminology. (I call it that, because I think it was one of America's "crusades.")
Churches were very slow in awakening to their responsibilities and many of them today are still not furnish-
ing the necessary leadership that could help alleviate
a great number of the problems. There has been some
change in the attitude of churches in the last few
years. The response of white churches in Atlanta at
the time of Dr. King's funeral was a very heartening
experience. I saw things at that occasion that I had
not seen before. Perhaps this is an indication of a
renewed attitude.

QUESTIONER: What is your feeling about the Task Force*
and its relevance to the black community and about the
objections against it now that it is predominantly
black?

MAYOR ALLEN: The police chief knows that he can more
effectively supervise certain Negro communities by
utilizing Negro policemen. But, we get into the
question of whether that isn't segregating the police
force. The Chief, of course, has desegregated the
force on several occasions. From an administrative
viewpoint, in carrying out a completely integrated
policy, you create some problems that you did not
anticipate.

---

*A special detachment of Atlanta police, mostly
black, created by Police Chief Herbert Jenkins to
respond quickly and with ethnic sensitivity to events
within predominantly black areas.

I can give you another example in the school
problem in Atlanta today. There are 25 schools in the
system of 105 at the present time that were all
that were integrated 25 to 30 percent with Negro
pupils, and that have now gone all Negro. This is not
integrating the school system, but the effort was made.
I am giving you some examples which prove that even
when the administrative intent is good these problems
may occur.

QUESTIONER: Is the city taking any measures to alleviate police brutality?

MAYOR ALLEN: Yes: examination, re-checking, checking
up. Jenkins is a man who has been the most liberally-
oriented police chief in America. He is the oldest
major city police chief who has survived these past
twenty years, and that is probably due to his liberal
orientation. He has tried to fully integrate his force.
There are dozens of openings on it right now to be
filled merely by application, and black and white
doesn't mean a thing. The question of police brutality
is one that we're checking into all the time. The
charges, about 99 out of 100, are not correct. There
is every effort being made to eliminate it completely,
however.

QUESTIONER: Do you forsee the rurally-oriented state
legislatures having distinct changes of attitude?

MAYOR ALLEN: Yes. We have more urban legislators now,
but many are new and naive. (I know a lot more about
running the Mayor's office today than I did when I went
in it eight years ago. I might not have gone in it had
I known what I know today!) But there is change in
both the composition and direction of the legislature
in a state such as Georgia. The Governor's recent tax
proposal, which was directly rurally oriented, five
years would have passed. This time it was defeated,
because there is an urban bloc which is looking out for

the interests of the cities. That bloc is not yet
strong enough to pass legislation, but it is strong
enough to align itself and defeat legislation! This is
a tremendous step forward. You have an active force of
new urban legislators getting some experience, people
with strong qualifications who are learning how "the
system" operates.

QUESTIONER: Will such legislature change affect the
race problem directly?

MAYOR ALLEN: The direction of state legislatures is
going to alter very rapidly as the urban entries take
over. The 1970 census will see major changes in the
present composition of state legislatures, and this
will give the urban centers a significant voice. The
good intentions of the American people and their basic
desires for a democratic society will be sustained by
such realignments. I think the race issue, by 1980,
will be pretty much out of the way. We will end it.
The next generation, not my children but my children's
children or my youngest children, is not going to have
the inhibitions, the violent attitudes or misunder-
standings that my generation has in regard to the race
issue.

QUESTIONER: Have the recent racially-oriented riots
been wholly detrimental to urban progress?

MAYOR ALLEN: The riots set us back ten years in eliminating racial discrimination; ten years! I really
think that! They accomplished some things of an
immediate nature but set the overall attitudes back.
They made it nearly impossible for those of us who had
worked together to try to establish an integrated
society: they put us in a defensive position. The
problems of the cities continue to be racially-oriented
issues.

QUESTIONER: I would like to know how integration

affects the school teacher. In some state where you have had desegregation, many black teachers who were principals of schools have been fired and replaced by white principals.

MAYOR ALLEN: I don't think you will see discrimination of that type in your central-city systems. Those have been rural systems. I think this has happened and may continue to happen in rural areas.

There can't be any question that the success of the Negro citizen as a full participant in Atlanta is aided and abetted by the fact that he has a substantial vote. The intelligent utilization of that vote will mute more discrimination than anything I know of. I see this happening every day in city government.

QUESTIONER: It is said that one of the causes for disorder in the country is because of an existing conflict between the oppressed and the oppressor or the "haves" and the "have-nots". It is also stated that Atlanta has some of the richest black people, "black bourgeoisie," in the nation. Would you consider this black affluence to be a major reason why Atlanta remained somewhat peaceful, especially after the assassination of Dr. Martin Luther King?

MAYOR ALLEN: I think there are a number of factors, no one of which would be the entire answer. I expect the single greatest reason has been this educational complex here which poured into Atlanta, more than any other city in the nation, a tremendous number of highly educated Negro citizens. Harlem and other places like it didn't have this influence. These black educators were a constructive force in demanding civil rights and equal opportunity but with a basic understanding that they could accomplish that faster in an orderly rather than in a disorderly way. If you pinned me down to the single greatest factor,

I would attribute it to the Atlanta University complex.
Further, out of this came a huge Negro business
community in Atlanta which doesn't exist anywhere else
in the nation on a comparable basis. Banks, building
and loan associations, professional people, and real
estate dealers, etc. No other Negro community in the
nation has it, and this was a contributing factor
through the years to aid Atlanta toward a more progressive effort.

The white business community of Atlanta continued
some communication, even when it was very difficult,
with this leadership of the Negro community of the city.

QUESTIONER: Why is it that the news media, radio, T.V.,
and the newspapers, seem to give wide coverage to white
events, but not to black?

MAYOR ALLEN: I am not going to agree with you!
In the position I am in, I hear the other side. I hear
the racists in Atlanta complain that the Atlanta newspapers don't ever print anything except about Negro
people anymore. I hear both sides. I have noted a
marked increase in the coverage of the Negro community
of Atlanta in the last year. A year ago, under the old
setup, there were no society items of the Negro
community. There were no feature pages. Every one of
them now is incorporated. It may not yet be equal,
totally equal, but there has been a predominant change.

QUESTIONER: How serious and successful can a white,
southern mayor really be in confronting racial issues?

MAYOR ALLEN: We whites were raised in a rigid system
and got into a field that was, for us, totally un-
chartered. There wasn't even a paper pamphlet on how
to solve this racial issue. I finally went to
Washington in '63 and testified, when Kennedy asked me
to, on the Civil Rights Bill. I was the only person
from the south who did go and testify, the only white

elected official. We had wallowed for five years trying to resolve this issue on a local basis of hotels,
restaurants, theatres, buses, parks, swimming pools,
but we had not satisfactorily resolved what had to be
solved.

The Negro community of Atlanta asked me not to
testify. Twenty-one of the twenty-five leading Negro
citizens in Atlanta said, "You are not going to pass
the Bill by testifying on it, and your going to get
the sock and stocking beat off of you in the next
election, and we don't want to lose you". I did
testify on behalf of it. I came back to a holocaust
in Atlanta from the white community. Six months
later, they changed their position entirely and said,
"You have done the right thing!" It was the best
thing I've ever done. Of course, we had to find
national solutions to this issue; we couldn't solve
it wholly on a local basis. What I'm saying is I was
the only guy who went up there and who had been
personally involved in trying to solve it. I
listened to all this claptrap about constitutional
rights and all that. That's not claptrap, constitutional rights, but when you try to twist it to
say that you could be denied certain rights, it is
constitutional claptrap. And we - I'm not saying
"me" - we have provided the national legislation required to correct this issue. If we can hang on for
the next 8 or 10 years, it can take effect.

RADICAL STUDENTS AND THIRD WORLD REVOLUTION

Mark Rudd

The concept of the Third World has to do with
non-white peoples primarily, originally from underdeveloped areas such as most of Africa, most of the
countries of Latin America, and Asia; it refers to
people out of economically underdeveloped, non-indus-
trialized countries and regions.

When you talk about Third World, then, you talk
about two things. First: The countries outside of
the communist block and outside of the industrialized, capitalist areas of the United States and
Europe. That takes into account most of the southern
hemisphere. Except in Latin America, where there were
European settlers, most of those countries are not
white. The other aspect of the concept of Third World
is colonized peoples; colonized in the sense that
their economy, their political institutions, their
nations are dominated from the outside. In many ways,
a colony often has its culture decimated. That's
what I'm going to talk about: the Third World, and
the opposite of it, which is the colonizer; the colonized and the colonizer.*

---

*Mr. Rudd's choice of a subject which deals with
contemporary political complexities gives some evidence
of his orientation within the new left. As Jack Newfield acknowledges, the "New Radicalism is pluralistic,
amorphous, and multilayered ... In Berkeley there is

Now, I think that's the basic struggle which is
going on in the world: struggle between the colonized
and the colonizer; between the advanced, industrialized,
capitalist countries and the Third World countries.

This struggle is what's happening in Africa where
the African countries first tried to overthrow the direct political colonization by European countries and
now, to some extent, are trying to get rid of the secondary domination of their economies by U.S. and European capital. In Latin America, most of the countries
have been politically free for over a hundred years,
and yet every country in Latin America except Cuba is
dominated completely and thoroughly by the United
States. In Asia, the people of Vietnam are attempting
to control their own country, to own the land, to dis-
tribute land justly to the poor peasants. The United
States moved in a half a million troops to stop them
from doing this. That's a clear case of American aggression or imperialism. That's the word for it.

Now, at home, we're engaged in a Third World struggle, too. That Third World struggle has to do with
black people and what black people are going through;
and, secondly, the response of white radicals, people
like myself, like those who made the rebellion in

---

strong sex-drug-literary orientation. In New York
there is a politically sophisticated component. In the
South there is extra emphasis on the non-violent religious element." Rudd, former chairman of the Students
for a Democratic Society at Columbia University, New
York (and currently the national chairman), shares the
political concern of the eastern-based aspect of the
movement. For further analysis of the political-moral
levels of the New Radicalism, see A PROPHETIC MINORITY
by Jack Newfield who was a charter member of the S.D.S.
in the early 1960's and an assistant editor of The Village Voice.

Columbia.

The three people I've been studying that I wanted
to mention in relation to these struggles are W.E.B
DuBois, Malcolm X and Huey P. Newton. DuBois, most of
you should know.* He was kicked out of Atlanta University for being too radical around the turn of the
century. By too radical it was meant that he wrote
about and talked about black identity, the black culture, about a tradition of black resistance to being
colonized. He also talked about the true history of
the United States; how the United States was built by
black people; how the history of the United States is
really one of racial conflict; how the working people
of this country have been duped, like the poor whites
of the south thinking somehow they had it better than
the slaves, and how they went out and fought a civil
war for the tiny planter class, a tiny oligarchy.
These white people were duped and the black people were

----

*W.E.B. DuBois' book, THE SOULS OF BLACK FOLK,
has been called more history-making than historical inasmuch as it marked a moment in black American experience when the commonality and potential of the group
was forcefully expressed. Although published in 1903,
it is still considered the classic restatement of race
relations as it rejects the concept of the "Negro Problem" and defines the "gift of Spirit" of black people.
White sociologists, such as Gunnar Myrdal and Charles
Silberman, note that DuBois' own sociological observations remain of unusual pertinence; while blacks have
interpreted DuBois as their spiritual ancestor of
Malcolm and Cleaver. At Atlanta University, where he
initiated a program of black studies, Du Bois asserted
that scientific inquiry would not, alone, make for
social reform. Increasingly, then, his work and
writings combined the detachment of the scholar and, as
in THE SOULS OF BLACK FOLK, the passion of the prophet.

made to suffer brutally.

DuBois was, I believe, the greatest historian that
the United States has ever seen. I wonder, maybe someone could tell me, are any of his works studied in any
of the courses in Atlanta University, or in any of the
white schools here?

GENERAL RESPONSE: Yes!

MR. RUDD: DuBois' conflict was with Booker T. Washington
who ran Tuskegee. They got into quite a fight, and it
had to do with identity, racism.* I'm not going to say
any more about DuBois. I think probably most of you
know more about him than I do. But he was a revelation,
because of the insight he had about the United States
and about American history.

The second person I've been reading is Malcolm X.
Most people also know something about his life from his
autobiography: how he was a hustler in the ghettos, then
went to prison for a number of years and, in prison, was
converted to the nation of Islam, the so-called Black
Muslims who follow the teachings of the life of Muhammed.

He also went through further conversions, further
changes; and toward the end of his life in 1963 and the
beginning of 1964, he broke with Elijah Mohammed and set
off on his own. One of the things he did during that
time was to spend most of the year 1964 in Africa. He
studied the revolutions that were taking place in Africa.

---

*An account of the differences, as well as similar-
ities, between Washington and DuBois may be found in
DuBois' essay "Of Mr. Booker T. Washington and Others"
in THE SOULS OF BLACK FOLK. The approach expressed by
Mr. DuBois was incorporated in the charter of the
Niagara Movement eighteen months later; that Movement
became the forerunner of the N.A.A.C.P.

He had some interesting observations about certain
things like the black revolution in the United States,
and about the need for militancy, the need sometimes
even for violence to achieve freedom.

He didn't have a worked-out plan. He didn't know
how to get there. But in many ways, he was really a
bold step forward. Two things he did; first, he talked
about self defense. And second, he tied up what was
going on here with the anti-colonial struggles in
Africa and throughout the Third World, the non-white,
underdeveloped countries.

One thing he said that really struck me comes from
a long passage in a speech he gave three months before
his death. He talked about the fact that the Congo,
since the end of Belgian rule, had been fought over by
the European and American mining interests; that the
Congo was extremely valuable to the industrialized
countries as a source of uranium, diamonds and cobalt,
and that industrialized countries like the United States
and the countries of Western Europe desperately needed
the Congo for its wealth. He continues with a long description on the wealth of the Congo and how, on the one
hand, the European powers and the United States fought
over this wealth and how a puppet, Tshombe, was eventually set up who represented European interests in the
Congo.

He ends up by saying: "I say this," meaning the
whole discussion of the real, key significance of the
Congo in the American and European economy, "I say this
because it is necessary for you and me to understand
what is at stake. You can't understand what is going
on in Mississippi if you don't understand what is going
on in the Congo. And you can't really be interested in
what's going on in Mississippi if you're not also
interested in what's going on in the Congo. They're
both the same. The same interests are at stake. The
same sides are drawn up. The same schemes are at work

in the Congo that are at work in Mississippi; the same
stake, no difference whatsoever."*

What he's referring to is the fact that the United
States or, rather, those who control the United States
plunder the Congo and need to dominate it, to colonize
it, to keep it under control. And what he's talking
about by analogy is that the situation in Mississippi
and Georgia and throughout the country is one of an internal colony of black people who have to be kept controlled, have to be exploited. Their labor has to be
exploited all the way from the tenant farmers in south
Georgia to the unemployed people in the ghettos of
Newark to the Black GI's of Vietnam. They have to be
used.

The third person I've been reading and finding out
about is Huey P. Newton. He is the founder of the Black
Panther party which originated in California. Recently,
the Black Panthers have been undergoing tremendous attack, a real attack from the Federal Government and from
the local State and Municipal Governments, from police
departments, from the courts, etcetera. 18 people in
the last year have been killed, 18 members of the Black
Panther party. Several dozen are in prison, including

---

*Since Malcolm's assasination in 1965, several
major works have been published either as collections
of his speeches or as critiques of progressions in his
thinking. Mr. Rudd quotes here from a presentation
Malcolm made in 1964 entitled "At the Audubon" and incorporated into a book, MALCOLM X SPEAKS. George Breitman, who edited this work, has also written the later
volume, THE LAST YEAR OF MALCOLM X. In a sense they
are complimentary, both focussing upon the conclusion
of Malcolm's career during which he envisioned a
broadening revolution. A third volume of import is the
AUTOBIOGRAPHY OF MALCOLM X, edited by Alex Haley.

Huey P. Newton, himself. Eldridge Cleaver has been
forced to flee. And Bobby Seale, the chairman of the
party, is under indictment from the demonstrations in
Chicago. He had nothing to do with them except he made
a speech for 15 minutes. And, now, 21 leaders of the
Black Panther party in New York, the entire leadership,
have been indicted on a phoney bomb plot, conspiracy.
19, the same week, were indicted on a phoney conspiracy
in Chicago. Pretty much all over, the Black Panther
party is undergoing attack. What Huey Newton was talking about was the fact that black people have been
treated as colonial subjects; the youth stripped of
their culture and subjugated as a people. And, in response, he's talking about the revolution, the anti-
colonial revolution. What is happening throughout the
world is also an anti-colonial revolution, in Vietnam,
in Cuba, and in many of the coutries in Latin America
where there are guerilla movements, and in dark Asia
and Africa. Third World people are deciding, "Now, we
want contol of our country" or, as Newton ended up saying, "We want what's ours."

In brief, what happened in Columbia University and,
I think, what's happening more and more around the
country is that a number of radical white students have
decided they also are trapped in this system of imperialism. They also, in many ways, are affected by this
class society.

There were two demands for example that were the
focus of our action in Columbia. The first had to do
with building the gymnasium in Morningside Park; in the
only parkland in west Harlem on land stolen from the
people of Harlem by Columbia University, a private, predominantly white institution.

That issue, in itself, was symbolic of the entire
way Columbia University faced Harlem and faced Morningside Heights ... Harlem is just two blocks away ...
namely, a racist way! Columbia wanted to clean up the

neighborhood. Columbia wanted to get rid of quote undesirables end quote. It wanted to make the neighborhood around Columbia lily white because that's safe for
a white institution.

Now, Huey Newton knew of all this: this is a practice from President Kirk's office! In those documents,
Kirk and other administrators spoke about cleaning up
the neighborhood of undesirables. That's a code word,
"undesirables." It means minority peoples and poor
whites at home. It means racism. It's just like law
and order. It's the same. It's a code word that has
to do with repression. For Columbia and the community
around it, Columbia's expansion represented that institution's racism; although only one aspect of it, I might
add.

The students at Columbia were saying, "No, that institution can't be racist." This fight was led by
American militant lads, black students in Columbia and
the Students For A Democratic Society. The black students
seized Hamilton Hall. They held it. They said to us,
"We're going to hold it ourselves and we're going to
barricade and we're going to fight the police off when
they come, because we're going to make a stand as black
people fighting this racist institution." The white
kids were really forced to make a decision. We made a
decision to follow the lead of the black students in
support of this anti-racist struggle, in support of what
I consider to be just one aspect of an entire national
liberation movement.

The other main issue had to do with the war in
Vietnam. If you studied the newspapers closely you get
some indication of what went on. Otherwise, nothing at
all came through except some vague idea of student
power.* But it had nothing to do with student power or

---

*Newspapers and mass-circulation periodicals showed

democratization of Columbia. It had to do with racism,
Columbia's racism, and Columbia's support for the war in
Vietnam; Columbia's support for the entire foreign policy
in the United States which radicals and Marxists and revolutionaries all over the world call imperialism.

We said that what Columbia was doing was developing
weapons for the Pentagon. Most of the weapons are coun-
ter-insurgency weapons to be used against guerilla movements such as the movement in Vietnam or the one in
Bolivia. Some of the weapons developed by the Institute
for Defense Analysis are being used in Goa and in
Guatemala to fight guerillas there. The American government is engaged in fighting the radical movements. It's
doing this in order to maintain its economic and political control over the Third World, the underdeveloped
countries.

Thus, there's a tremendous conflict in the world.
It's a war, and it's not only in Vietnam. It's in
dozens, literally dozens, of these underdeveloped
countries where people are getting together very slowly
and running tremendous risks of getting together to kick
the United States out.

This is certainly what happened in Cuba. The Cuban
economy was completely dominated, completely exploited
by the United States. Almost half the sugar plantations,
which were the main resource of Cuba, were owned by the

---

no acute interest in the issues of racism and war
and, as Rudd claims, concentrated their focus on the
success and failure of militancy among Columbia's
students. TIME's review used the word "hooligan" to
describe those who occupied President Kirk's office and,
without intention, may have complimented Mr. Rudd when
it stated, "The man most intent upon keeping the pressure on Columbia remains Mark Rudd. The day after his
suspension he was back haranguing students ...".

United States investors. The banks in Cuba were owned
by the United States. The telephone company, the electric company, the railroads, everything was the United
States.

The people in Cuba, those who had work in rural
areas, worked three months a year cutting cane. The
rest of the time they were unemployed. They lived in
mud or grass huts. They had no adequate diet. In fact,
many of them died of TB and parasites and other diseases
that have to do with underdevelopment. Since the revolution in Cuba, the Cuban government and the Cuban people
have been engaged in a process of building up their
country.

Now, I was very fortunate in that I went to Cuba in
February, 1968. I was there for only about three weeks,
but in that time, I saw they had built hospitals and
built roads, and concrete houses and replaced the grass
houses, the shacks and huts. In the rural areas, people
had schools; people had jobs, productive labor, and were
working to build up the country. Agricultural production
was much higher. In almost every way, Cuban people were
building up their country; were living decent human
lives. Of course, there are dissatisfied people. But
many, many people I spoke to, and I speak Spanish somewhat, said, "Yes, life is so much better now under
socialism." The reason they felt this way was they knew
they were all working to build up their country, and
they were being effective.*

----

*Mr. Rudd's analysis of the Cuban economy corre-
lates closely with that of the late Che Guevara who em-
phasized, like Rudd, the general success of Cuban
"planification" (Che's term) despite transitional er-
rors. Che's major thesis was that man's will to create
is the necessary premise on which the socialist political and economic structures depend and, further, that
the objective conditions present at a time and place

It's the same way in almost all the other underdeveloped countries, the Third World countries that are
socialist. In North Vietnam, before it was destroyed by
American bombs, in Korea, in China; these countries have
all undergone tremendous development, much greater than
similar countries in that area.

For example, just one statistic: In the years 1950
to 1960, according to CIA figures, the rate of economic
and agricultural growth in China was 10 percent per year
in that 10 year period. Now, that includes droughts and
rainstrorms and famines, et cetera. In India, the rate
of economic growth, industrial and agriculture was 3%.
So, the rate of growth, the building up of the country,
the well-being of the people in China was growing at a
rate of three times that of India. Just one fact.

In almost all the countries of Latin America, at
least the ones outside Chile and Argentina and Uruguay,
starvation is the rule. In all the countries, poor
health facilities are the rule. In Brazil, 60 percent
of the people ·are illiterate. In Cuba, 50 percent of
the people were illiterate. That's no longer true.

At the same time, all these countries have wealth,
and all of them are places of investment for American
business such as the tremendous amounts of capital in-

----

must fashion the peculiarities of particular
socialist systems. In a candid speech entitled "On
the Cuban Experience", Che noted that Cuban development
was slower than necessary because of early attempts to
imitate brother revolutionary experiments, the result
being a continuing problem with bureaucratism. But,
according to Che, the capitalist neocolonial state was
destroyed, and the bases of an economy resting dis-
tinctly on Cuban production possibilities was established.

vested by the oil companies. Examples are the American
Oil Company and some European oil companies in
Venezuela. The rate of return on Standard Oil capital
in Venezuela is about three times that of the rate of
return of similar investments, say, in Texas or Okla-
homa. There's about 1.1 billion dollars capital invested in Venezuela. The amount of return on that
investment is 225 million dollars, a little less than
one quarter. In the United States, rates of return
average eight and ten percent. So, there are tremendous
profits being made from these countries, from the tremendous wealth in their oil and the natural resources. But
at the same time, the people are growing more miserable,
poorer and poorer. That's one aspect of it.

Another aspect of imperialism I'd like to emphasize
is the military part. In Santo Domingo in 1965 there
was a reform regime elected, led by Juan Bosch. The
regime was constitutional, and promised land reform. In
1965, right after the election, President Johnson sent
11,000 marines into the Dominican Republic to topple the
democratic reform government and install a military
junta. That is American diplomacy. That is American
imperialism. That's no unique case.

600,000 G.I.s in Vietnam. North Vietnam and South
Vietnam both are bombed continuously. Now, they've
stopped bombing North Vietnam after they've destroyed
it completely. They still found the guerillas were
fighting, and that bombing did not stop the people of
North Vietnam from fighting back. In Thailand, the war
is beginning now. There are 40,000 American troops
there. In Laos, the war has been hushed up for several
years, but there's guerilla action there. In fact, all
over the world, the United States is using military
means to put down either reformers, as in the past
regimes of the Dominican Republic, or present revolutionary regimes or movements as in Vietnam.

That's the external aspect of American imperialism.

It is in such tiny countries that the American military
is overextended all throughout the world. It's not an
accident that the U.S. has close to a thousand bases in
60 countries throughout the world. It's in order to
maintain control over this empire, this so-called "free
world." That's the word which is used.

Take a look at this "freedom" in a country such as
Brazil. The fact is that there is no freedom at all, no
constitutional government, no freedom of speech, press,
assembly, anything. This may be compared with Cuba
where you can speak your mind, where people are elected
to the communist party, and where the communist party
tries to be responsive to the needs of the people. I'm
not defending Cuba completely, but I think you have to
compare apples with apples and oranges with oranges. A
lot of us have fears of communism built into us where we
shrink back from new concepts such as the socialist society attempted in Cuba.

Now, internally in the United States, what is imperialism doing? It is forcing many young people to go
and fight in Vietnam. So, there has been the rise of
the draft resistance movement. Or, at home, it's
forcing more and more people, working people, to pay a
15 percent surtax. At home there's no more money for
education. I understand there's a welfare freeze in
Alabama. Is that correct?

A VOICE: In Georgia!

MR. RUDD: In Georgia, hmm. In New York City, which has
the highest prices of any city in the country the welfare allotment per child per day for food has gone down
from 85¢ to 60¢ per day. In New York City, the schools
are running three shifts a day. In New York City, they
need approximately 25 new high schools just to maintain
a classroom size of 20 students per classroom. They
need 25 new high schools, but they have none slated because there is no money. And yet, 80 billion dollars

or more is going for defense. More and more G.I.'s are
employed in that. One out of every seven jobs in the
United States is involved with either the military or
production for the military. And yet, there is such a
tremendous need in our cities.

There are the needs of hospitals: In New York City,
I've been at one of the hospitals in the Bronx. It
serves 250,000 people. The hospital is known in Spanish
- this is a Puerto Rican neighborhood - as the butcher
house, and people just will not go there. They'd rather
die at home than in the butcher house. The maternity
ward has been closed for the last few months because of
the rate of vaginal infection and the rate of infection
in newborn babies. There aren't facilities to clean it
up or for doctors to provide adequate care. That's
Lincoln Hospital in the Bronx. All over the country,
public health care is a disgrace. Yet, Cuba, a tiny
little country, has money for health care. America does
not.*

Another aspect of imperialism at home we all have
just gone through is called the Wallace movement. And
if you talk to some Wallace people one thing that you
find is that they are really uptight about a number of
other things beside race, and they have real problems.
One of them is high taxes. They've had no say in
government and yet more and more of their wages go for

_____

*In 1967, the Statistical Office of the United
Nations revealed that there were seventeen countries
in the world which had better infant mortality records
than that of the United States and that, in the United
States, there was a loss of approximately 40,000 lives
per year as a consequence. And yet, in that same year,
the new President of the American Medical Association
declared in his opening address that "The United States
(has) a quality of health care unsurpassed anywhere".

taxes. They're unhappy about it. The liberal politicians have nothing to say to that except, "Give more
and more money for taxes." Wallace on the other hand
gave a phoney solution. He said, "Your money is going
for welfare," while the real answer is that the money
is going to support imperialism, to finance imperialism.

The point I am making about the Wallace movement
is that there is real discontent even among the white
people who have many privileges, who have in many cases
had privileges in relation to blacks. For example,
black people are the last hired and the first fired in
factories. Black people have the less skilled jobs.
White people get more skilled jobs and get advancement.
That's a rule in factories, both in the north and the
south. Whites have accepted such privileges. Whites
have been oppressors of the black people. The privileged whites, however, have lost, too. What they've
lost is the knowledge and understanding of who the enemy
is; who really is responsible for the war in Vietnam;
who benefits from it; who gets rich off the war industries; who has been pushing the war in Vietnam. In a
sense, they've lost the ability to unite with black
people who are also working people to hit out at the
real enemy. And I'm going to call this real enemy, by
a piece of Marxist rhetoric, "the ruling class." This
small class of people, 2,000 families, it is estimated,
control approximately 70 percent of the productive
wealth of this country. 2,000 families!

Now, many workers have been fed a bill of goods.
Many black people have been fed a bill of goods.
They've been fed lies and they've accepted them about
the opportunities in the society, about progress in this
society being inevitable, about upward mobility for
everyone. But the fact of the matter is that such "progress" is not working out for working people. It is not
working out for black people. In saying this, I'm trying to build a case for the revolution, and get down to
some facts. One thing that has falsely bolstered this

country for so long is what I'd call the myth of progress. White working class people say, "Well, my son
will be in the middle class. My son will have the
wealth." Or, "Day by day the unions are giving me more
and more."*

The sons of working class people in any of our
cities are finding out that the only education opportunities that are open to them are junior colleges,
community colleges. And the junior colleges teach you
mostly about jobs that will soon be obsolete, like data
processing and typing up punch cards. Computers are
going to handle that, but that's what's taught in junior
colleges. After many of the vocational courses in junior colleges, there won't be any more need for these
people. Sons of working class people, white and black,
will be unemployed.

Black people; you know since civil rights there
have been so many dreams about how things are getting
better. Recently, however, certain statistics were revealed by the Bureau of Statistics and were published
in the New York Times. (I don't trust the New York
Times, but these statistics are against the interests
of those people who control the New York Times.) The
statistics say that in every aspect of the material
well-being of people: jobs, housing, education, health,
unemployment; in every aspect, the gap between white and

----

*The myth of socio-economic mobility in America is
a strange amalgamation of economic liberalism and Darwinian theories of evolutionary progress. As Mr. Rudd implies, the American business elite have been recruited
mostly from the preceding upper classes, and this process of recruitment has remained stable. Studies by
Reisman, Seymour Lipset and others confirm that the
ideology of economic equalitarianism has been more a
part of frontier folklore than fact.

black has been growing between 1950 and 1965.

One aspect of life, the one most important indicator of material well-being with people, is that of infant mortality. That one indicator reveals not only that the gap between white and black is growing, but the rate for black people is also growing. The rate of infant mortality has been great, generally, in the richest country in the world, according to the Bureau of Labor Statistics, but the rate for black people, between 1950 and 1965, was growing greater. Now, this is covered up, of course. Many of us don't see it, and it is certainly not in the papers normally; but it is true.

This country is not doing what it has to do, because so much of its wealth is going to imperialism. Imperialism is not benefitting people of the United States as it has in years past. The plunder of the Third World brought wealth here. Well, that's just not so any more. The plunder of the Third World is now a very costly operation: it's taking wealth from the working people and putting it in the pockets of the ruling class.

Now, what happens at schools? What happened among white students is that they got uptight about what their jobs are used for, their lives are used for, and their careers. As the students at Columbia said, "God, what are we going to do after we leave school? Are we going to be part of this system? Are we going to be managers? Are we going to be exploiters? Are we going to be officers in the military? What are we going to do?"

They felt a tremendous alienation, boredom, whatever it is, malaise, about school.* All you have to do

----

*A scholarly exploration into this "tremendous alienation" has been made by Kenneth Keniston in his book, YOUNG RADICALS: NOTES ON COMMITTED YOUTH. He

is go over and talk to students at Emory or Georgia
State or probably Atlanta University and maybe, deep
down inside they feel this tremendous malaise; they
also see the problem of the ideology of universities,
namely, this is supposed to be some place for the pursuit of rational truth.

At Georgia State, people are being trained to be
middle level managers; or at Emory, people are being
trained to be professionals and to work for their future employers. I'm not familiar with Atlanta University and different parts of it, but you can probably
see the similarities. Probably you can tell me a lot
about it. Engineers, for example, are trained to work
in defense industries. Many of the engineers that are
trained in Atlanta go to Lockheed. Now, almost none of
this has to do with filling the needs of the people of
this country or the world; very little of it.

Architects at Columbia, for example, went on strike.
They were the only group there, as a professional group,
to go on strike. They said, "No. We find it impossible
to study architecture at Columbia. We know it would be

---

discusses the personal roots of struggle, the life
periods of radicalization, and the variety of emotions
experienced by those who identify with Movement work.
Although for different reasons which come out of a different perspective, Kentston agrees with Rudd's feeling
that alienation among American youth will be a continuing phenomenon. He also claims that it will be the
most talented, sensitive persons who will reject the
society which repells them. According to Keniston, society does not need to accept responsibility toward the
cure of those alienated, since alienation does not need
"cure"; instead, the social order should provide productive means through which youthful and other alien-
ations may be expressed.

impossible to practice architecture in the future; to build buildings for human use; to rebuild the cities, because the interests of profit, the interests of capital get in the way. They decide what kind of buildings we are going to build, what kind of cities we are going to plan."

This is one example of the irrationality of imperialism. It's completely irrational to build cities with miles and miles of highways through them and over them and under them. It's completely irrational. What cities need is mass public transportation. I can get on the subway and reach a destination in a few minutes. It's cheap. It's clean. It doesn't pollute the air. The only thing it does not also do is, it doesn't consume more cars. Mass public transportation doesn't consume more tires, more oil, more steel. The economy has created the need for more and more consumption, so now we have our cities completely fucked up with highways, and the air is completely polluted. The reason is because of the needs of profit, not the needs of human beings. It is totally irrational, irrational!

Automotive engineers don't design cars that are safe or cars that will last. They design cars that will wear out in two years. Everybody knows that that's the nature of the system. So, people go along with it, and they pay tremendous loans and credit. They pay interest on credit to pay off the cars, notes, too. People want the cars, etc.

QUESTIONER (Interrupts Mr. Rudd): You've been talking about the evils of capitalism, and yet I'm not completely satisfied that a socialistic, state-run system can be much better. Why wouldn't it, eventually, run into red tape where we, as citizens, would be getting directions from some committee that made the decisions? I don't see how you can communicate in a nationwide socialist system.

MR. RUDD: Well, to some extent you can't; but it's more

possible in socialism. Socialism involves the decentral-
ization of decisions. For example: In China, they do
decentralize many decisions at a factory level. What I
am trying to do here is to settle the groundwork for the
necessity of the inevitability of socialism.

DIALOGUE WITH MARK RUDD

QUESTIONER: Now, you talk about revolution. What do
you mean by revolution? Do you think you can have this
democratic revolution peacefully?

MR. RUDD: First of all, the revolution is developing in
the black movement through the Panthers and many other
groups around the country; and it's developing in mass
movements like certain workers' movements. There's one
in Detroit called The Revolutionary Union Movement of
Black Workers in Auto Plants who, basically, are fighting racism in the shops and are also talking about the
needs of socialism. All of these movements are democratic. All of them are mass movements. They seek to
build in such a way that they serve the needs of the
people. They don't serve the needs of an elite.

     For example: I don't want to be President in social-
ism. Nor does SDS want to rule socialism. Nor does the
party. But, rather, the mass democratic movement we're
building in SDS and these other organizations and the
new ones to come will be the basis for the institutions
of socialism.

     As far as the way the revolution is going to take
place, I think that it's inevitable that the ruling
class in this country is not going to give up easily.
Black people, for example, have not been able to obtain
freedom, and they've found that they've had to defend
themselves, and sometimes even give an aggressive attack.
I think of the example in Vietnam. The Vietnamese people

have not been able to win non-violently. From the
years 1955 to 1960, they did not engage in guerilla
warfare against the enemy. They tried to overthrow
Diem peacefully. It did not work.

And in the United States, I think you'll find that
the ruling class would rather use repression and violence against the revolutionary movement to seize the
means of production, to seize the industries, to seize
the government, even if it were a majority. Now, there
was a majority of the country, I believe, supporting
McCarthy. Yet those who control the Democratic Party
ran Humphrey. McCarthy had tremendous rapport. I was
not, myself, for McCarthy, but he was a peace candidate.
But the power structure, the control of the Democratic
Party, would not allow this majority candidate to even
come close to nomination. They completely sewed him
up. All you had to do was turn on the television and
watch it.

At Columbia we took some physical force. Yes,
it's true we occupied buildings in order to stop Columbia's racist expansion, in order to stop its support
for war and imperialism in Vietnam. And the response
was not negotiation. It was not, "Yes, we'll meet your
demands because they're just." And they clearly were
just demands. It was, rather, to call in the cops and
beat us up and bust us and throw a number of people out
of school. The response to the revolutionary movement
here has been assassination and jailment. The response
to Malcolm X, the man who spoke about black identity,
was assassination.

Now, I wish the revolution could take place peacefully. I really wish it, but it's not going to be.
It's like Mick Jagger, the famous philosopher from the
Rolling Stones said. Somebody asked him what he thought
about the Beatles song, "Revolution," the one that's
sort of a pacifist song. He replied, "Well, they,"
meaning the Beatles, "they think that a song can make a
revolution."

I wish it could. I wish non-violence here could
make a revolution, but I think the power structure is
violent enough; it has enought arms; it has enough guns;
it's willing enough to use them, that the minute we step
out of line, they'll really hit us with it hard. That's
already happened. They also have the courts. For example: I'm facing two years in proson for a riot charge, a
trumped up charge. And the Black Panthers are facing 20
years in prison on trumped up charges of conspiracy to
blow up department stores in the Bronx, black peoples
department stores.

QUESTIONER: To what extent can a student action movement ever mean anything? For example: We've had an
action movement going for several months, and yet it
seems to me that all I can see ahead is ultimate failure.

MR. RUDD: I don't know the terms of ultimate settlement,
but I think they did get a black studies movement going,
and they got opportunities for oriental people and
others at San Francisco State. So, in some ways, it was
a success. Also, at Columbia, we won on IDA. Columbia
was disaffiliated from the Institute of Defense Analysis.
And, we stopped the gym. On the other hand, Columbia is
still expanding in the neighborhood, and they plan to
send 10,000 people out of their homes in the next eight
years; and Columbia is still doing experiments, some of
them in chemical and biological warfare.

So, at Columbia we didn't win in our broader aims.
But we did win in the sense that we built the basis for
a movement. We radicalized people. We got across our
analysis of the university being controlled and used by
the ruling class.

Real lasting reforms such as a free university, I
don't believe, will be possible because the ruling class
would rather shut down the universities than to allow
them to become completely free in the sense of serving
the needs of the people. For example, again at San

Francisco State, they did shut down the university before they would have a completely autonomous black
studies institute. They need the university to train
personnel, to develop skills, and to fuck over people's
minds. That's what the universities are for!

I really think there's a contradiction between
what the ruling class uses universities for and the
fact that we want a completely free society, one in
which people's needs are met because they are human
beings, one in which people can develop their potential. And that contradiction is really the final contradiction that is going to build socialism, but not a
free university. So, negotiations are really a very
difficult task, because the power structure is not going
to negotiate what's needed.

QUESTIONER: You said your talk would be on the Third
World, and I gather that the Third World means, from
what you said, those persons or countries that are not
white or American; and, let's say, capitalistic. You
named countries in Latin America, Africa, and northern
Asia. But, how will we talk about people of the Third
World repressed by the United States and at the same
time forget such countries that are included in the
Warsaw Pact, as Czechoslovakia, Hungary, Roumania and
Poland? I would like to ask, isn't the action that took
place in Czechoslovakia a few months ago and that which
took place in Hungary in 1956, the same thing you are
accusing the United States of doing to other countries?

MR. RUDD: It's obviously true that the Soviet bloc represents one major force, but it's a different kind of
force. Now, I'm not going to be put in a position of
defending the Soviet Union. I think it's totalitarian.
I think it's going very much in the wrong direction and
doing very many brutal things. But the Soviet Union
does not have one penny of capital invested outside of
the eastern European countries. The Soviet Union is not
exploiting these Third World countries. It's the United

States that's doing this.

These Third World countries form the basis of the
American empire. They also form the theatre in which
the United States is aggressive. For example: The
United States has been aggressive in Greece, and the
United States has been aggressive in Vietnam. The
United States has been attempting to control these
countries that are fighting for freedom.

The conflicts between the Soviet Union and its
satellites, I think, are very much secondary. Important, but still secondary to the fact of American imperialism. You see, in some ways the Soviet bloc, the
Soviet sphere of influence, is a response to a very aggressive American policy after World War II. I would
like to refer you to a story by Horowitz and Carl Oglesby when they talk about the cold war, especially in
Oglesby's book, *Containment and Change*. That volume
speaks about the cold war as being a result of aggressive American foreign policy, and of Stalin's reaction
by holding a buffer zone, satellites that serve as a
defense against western aggression.

Also, the Soviet Union is extremely terrified of
the resurgence of an aggressive imperialist West Germany. That's important, too. So, the Soviet Union was
really scared that Czechoslovakia was going to go toward
West Germany. The Soviet Union had been for a long time
terrified of war. Now, certainly, the Soviet Union has
other aims, too, in controlling the communist countries
of eastern Europe. The Soviet Union wants to sell its
goods, realize property, get manufactured goods from
eastern Europe. But all of this, I believe, is completely secondary to the main thrust of contemporary
history which is the conflict between the United States
and some of its allies and Third World countries.

In some ways, the totalitarianism and the defens-
iveness of the Soviet Union and its bloc is the result

of an aggressive United States and expansion of the
United States empire.

There are going to have to be revolutions in the
Soviet Union and in the eastern European countries also.
And I think those revolutions will happen as the revolutions in the Third World countries progress. It's
going to be the revolutions in the Third World countries
that start our movement, that have already started it.
It's going to be the revolutions in the Third World
countries such as Vietnam that start a resurgence of
socialism in these bureaucratic and elitest countries
of the Soviet bloc.

Everyone I knew who passed through the latter
stages of the civil rights movement say that it is the
Third World thinkers and revolutionaries they look to
for guidance and for understanding. Certainly, this was
the case of Malcolm X and the case of Huey Newton and
the Panthers. It's no accident that the upsurgence of
the civil rights movement in the U.S. was parallel and
simultaneous to the upsurgence of the anti-colonial
struggles in Africa.

These Third World anti-imperialist fights started
something going in the United States. I think for white
revolutionaries, the example of black people, the example of the people of the Third World, the Vietnamese,
their courage and determination and strength is really
an example that got us going. And now we're moving into areas, talking to working class people about working
class revolution, which I think will be the future emphasis.

QUESTIONER: What essential ingredient do you see in the
revolution in this country which would produce an ap-
preciatively different result from what is happening in
the Soviet Union?

MR. RUDD: I think I can point to one significant factor

that the United States has that no country in the world
had, that is, tremendous productive wealth. The wealth
to fit the needs of all the people of this country and
possibly of the whole world. Tremendous wealth almost
at our fingertips and yet we still don't have access to
it.

     The Soviet Union was a country that was really
backward in 1917. They've had to go through strains to
industrialize, and also to fight World War II and re-
cover from that event where over half of the industry
of the country was destroyed. The Soviet Union has had
to institute totalitarianism, and I condemn that. But
the United States has the potential for a really abun-
dant society, because the productive wealth is here.
We almost have production in our grasp without anybody
working, other than through cybernation, through computers.*

     We also have tremendous wealth in the country
that's not even used. For example: The production of
steel is at a level of about a half of what it was at
the end of World War II. The production of that basic
commodity, steel.

QUESTIONER: Doesn't your analysis, then, doom the
people of the Third World to repeat the Russian experi-
ment before they go through what's happening here?

_____

     *The science of cybernetics is variously defined
but ordinarily deals with the construction, manipulation
and application of models which represent the organization of physical entities such as brains or symbolic
entities such as information systems. Mr. Rudd's es-
pecial mention of computers in relation to cybernation
acknowledges the prolific use, in the United States in
particular, of varieties of mechanisms of "artificial
intelligence."

They're worse off in capital goods than the Soviets were in 1917!

MR. RUDD: No. The Third World is not bereft of capital. It has primary natural resources to industrialize and develop its countries. For example: Cuba has no energy fuels, it has nothing for industry; but it has very rich soil. And Cuba has been able to industrialize and build schools, highways, hospitals, et cetera by producing sugar which it sells abroad at a fairly good rate to the Soviet Union. The Soviet Union then sends in return for the sugar, machinery, productive machinery. As of now, Venezuela would be one of the richest countries in the world if its oil was owned by the people of Venezuela. Also, the Third World countries have resources that the so-called industrialized countries cannot do without. It's been estimated that 80 percent of the minerals in the jet engine come from Africa and Latin America and cannot be gotten elsewhere. If the United States paid a fair price, and if it sent industrial goods for these minerals, it would be able to help develop these countries through the purchase of their resources.

Now, there are problems in this. There are obvious problems such as the fact that there's going to have to be tremendous shifts in the world economy so that the United States and Japan and Western Europe, instead of producing all of the world's automobiles and other manu- factured goods, will engage in a division of labor with these other countries.

Perhaps in these shifts there would be dislocations, but it would not have to mean tremendous privation on the part of the Third World countries to make these shifts. As of now, it means war. As of now, economic development means war with the United States, and I think that's the worst dislocation that can possibly happen.

QUESTIONER: I have trouble seeing an association of the

SDS movement with the Black Panther movement. I have
trouble associating Malcolm X with a Third World attack
against imperialism since Malcolm X and the Black Muslims would have a tendency to feel that we blacks are
now representing the Third World!

I tend to see in the SDS an attempt to use the
black power movement to follow idealistic goals which
happen not to be immediate goals in the black revolution. As for closing the colleges and sticking the
SDS label on the black movement, I simply fail to find
the identification between its goals and our black
goals.

MR. RUDD: In looking at the Black Panther policy which
stresses land, housing, jobs, freedom, et cetera, most
people would feel that this is one which states the
goals of the larger black movement. In this program,
revolutionaries like Huey P. Newton have said something
like the following: "Besides developing a national liberation movement in the colony, we, meaning the Panthers,
are stirring a revolutionary movement in the mother
country. And, just logically speaking, it would seem
impossible to me, absolutely impossible to me that my
people would achieve these goals: housing, freedom,
through capitalism."

I think SCLC, Panthers, Snick, and some others recognize that it's capitalism that needs to maintain the
black people as a colony. Now, my goal is freedom for
all people. I think that can be said to be the goal of
SDS.

QUESTIONER: We blacks do feel strong identification
with what you might term the anti-imperialistic move,
but not so much from the same goals you would have.
Ours are not a total idealism of a perfect economy but
come from the fact that we are a racial minority. We
identify worldwide with the kind of movement that would
give us nationalism so as to tend to make us a basic

majority.

MR. RUDD: All over the world there are nationalist
movements, as you say. There are nationalist movements,
as in Vietnam. It is a nationalist movement, but it is
also a socialist movement because the people of Vietnam
understand that they cannot possibly obtain freedom from
the United States' exploitation without kicking American
capital out and also creating a socialist system within
that country.

     Now, I don't see how black people at home in the
United States, in the mother country, really in the
heart of the monster, so to speak, are going to attain
jobs and peace and land and housing and freedom and
justice without a major revision of the exploitive system that is responsible.

QUESTIONER: How will a white fit into the black power
revolution? Why will he fit into a black revolt? What
is your motive?

MR. RUDD: Let me read a quote from Malcolm. That will
get the sum of it. This is after a speech Malcolm gave.
Someone says, "What political and economic system do
you want?" And his answer is, "I don't know, but I'm
flexible."

     As was stated earlier, all of the countries emerg-
ing today from under the shackles of colonialism are
turning toward socialism. I don't think it's an accident most of the countries that were colonial powers
were capitalist countries. And the last bulwark of
capitalism today is America. It's impossible for a
white person to believe in capitalism and not believe
in racism. You can't have capitalism without racism.
If you find one and you happen to get that person into
a conversation and they have a philosophy that makes
you sure they don't have this racism in their outlook,
usually they are socialists or their political

philosophy is socialism.

Now, as far as what whites are going to do: What
I'm going to do, and what I would like to hope others
in the white movement as a whole will do, is address
myself to whites; address myself to racists such as the
working class racists who have been sold lies for so
many years about their superiority, their supremacy over
blacks. They have somehow gotten privileges out of this,
but have also been used by the ruling class, by the capitalist class. That's what I think the white revolutionary movement should do.

Secondly: The revolutionary movement should attack
institutions, the racism of institutions, universities
like Columbia. It should attack the government's racism.
At Columbia, we talked to people about the privileges
they get out of the all-white university, and how that's
racism, and how much they're losing through that racism.
That's one aspect of what we should be doing.

If you've been through the army as some of my
friends have, you've noticed the way GI's talk about
Vietnamese people as "gooks", those little yellow people.
They don't treat them as human beings. They treat them
as yellow objects, gooks, who can be killed or murdered,
against whom genocide, bombing with napalm, etcetera is
a normal thing. Racist ideas on the part of American
whites are responsible for the maintainance of imperialism. You would never find napalm, you would never
find the atom bomb being used against Europe; but it was
used against the Japanese. You'd never find the genocide of an entire country such as happened in Vietnam
done to a European country; but it is done against a
yellow country. So, racism goes hand in hand with imperialism.

As far as what I'm in it for, I'll tell you. I can
only speak for myself. Possibly ideas I've had and
feelings I've had are similar to what young people,

white people like myself, have had. We've grown up in
a society which has such a tremendous gap between capability and realization; a gap in which there is so much
suffering; a gap in which we found all of our illusions
about peace and all of our illusions about rights, human
rights of people, dashed through the war in Vietnam and
through the failure of the civil rights movement, and
through the race situation and the exploitation of
blacks at home. We were tremendously disillusioned. We
were tremendously uptight, in a sense, because of all
the things that had happened.

I tried to say this before: what kind of jobs would
we be called on to do? If I had finished school, I
would have been a teacher. I would have gone to a university and indoctrinated a kid in traditional political
science ideas that had to do with lies, that were completely lies about progress and lies about the so-called
democratic system. That would have been my job. I
couldn't see a possibility for me in that job. The only
career I could see for myself was one of attempting to
be part of a movement that changes everything around,
because I could see that as the only justice for the human family. That's what I get out of it.

I think that other people are turning to this movement for similar reasons.

QUESTIONER: I agree with very much of what you said,
but I have certain qualms. I'd like to have certain
things explained. One of them is why are black leaders
supporting the United Arab nations against the
Israelis? It seems definitely inconsistent to me that
they can support the collective Arab countries which include those that have plundered Sudan. How can Carmichael or Brown accept money from these Arab nations
when racism is practiced by these same Arab nations?
Many Arab countries practiced genocide against the Sudan,
taking people out as slaves. On the other hand, Israel,
for a non-black nation, has the highest ratio of black

students to students of their country of any non-black
nation in the world.

MR. RUDD: I don't know about the Sudan. I would tend
to doubt that revolutionary leaders of the black liberation movement would consciously, knowingly support a
racist and a sell-out government like the one you described. I do know that the black leaders have denounced Malawi because it has been pro-imperialist.
It trades with South Africa. It exploits the people at
home, recognizes Rhodesia, et cetera.

I think my position on Israel, and I think the position of most revolutionaries around the world, is not
so much support for Egypt or support for the government
of Egypt and some of the feudal governments of the Arab
countries; it is more a recognition that Israel has com-
mited certain crimes. For example: Two and a half million Palestinians, Arabs by and large, were displaced
from their land. If you talk about colonialism, that is
colonialism. They are in refugee camps. Their land was
taken by the Zionists, and they were sent out. The
Arabs who stayed at home are treated as subservient minorities. They are exploited economically. They are
held away. They do have some political rights but not
complete political rights.

Basically there is another way to look at the question, and this is important. How does Israel line up on
the problem of imperialism? What does Israel do?
Israel trades with South Africa, as does the United
States to whom it is tied. Israel recognizes South
Africa, and trades also with Rhodesia. Israel has not
helped the progressive Third World countries like
Tanganyika. It has helped some individuals in the
governments of countries that have undergone military
coups like Ghana. Although Israel has had certain experiments internally, externally it lines up completely
and thoroughly with the United States, the enemy of the
colonialized peoples around the world. One of the

reasons is that Israel's economy is dependent on the United States, on certain investments and on gifts from Zionists in the United States.

Now, I myself was born a Jew and I grew up in the tradition of thinking that the worst thing that had happened in this decade was the genocide against 6,000,000 Jews in Europe. But, on the other hand, I don't see why the Arabs have to pay for that genocide, and why a State has to be artifically established on land that belongs to other people, and that has belonged to them for several hundred years. Maybe it belonged to the Jews thousands of years ago, but before that, it belonged to the Canaanites, and if you're going to go way back, you don't know where to stop. For the intervening hundreds of years, there were the Palestinians, the Arabs. The Jews have come in and have attempted to take away their land. They have succeeded. They have established an artificial state there with American backing and with English backing.

I consider that state, incidentally, to be an inroad of imperialism in the Middle East. This is not to say that Saudi Arabia and Iran and, in some sense, Iraq and even Egypt and Algeria now and many other Arab countries are not controlled economically by imperialism. But, in these countries there are other aggressive movements.

I'm saying there's one touchstone, one criterion for whether a country is progressive or reactionary. Israel rates very badly.

QUESTIONER: I think this ties in with another question. The concept of "good white people" is of no help in the black revolution right now. I don't doubt that there probably are some of them, some whites who are serious about ending oppression, imperialism, the ghettos, helping the Third World underdeveloped nations. But, take the example of the Democratic Convention in Chicago with

its brutality, the kind that goes on here in Atlanta
day to day. What happened to all those white people
that got beat across the head? I'll tell you. They
went back and got in their Jaguars and drove away!

Where are they now? You see sporadic movements.
Maybe they have a week of remembrance of this somewhere.
I'm saying they cry with us; they march with us; they
sing with us; and they talk about our problems. But
when it comes to being out there on the street with us,
they may get their lumps one time and then you don't
see them anymore. They check out!

MR. RUDD: Would somebody like to answer this?

[At this point, responders from audience answered several questions - W.O.]

RESPONDER (white): I think it's one of the most crass
expressions I've heard all night, and I've heard some
pretty crass expressions! I'll tell you now, nobody in
those Chicago crowds had a Jaguar. Those people went to
sleep in Lincoln Park, because they didn't have any
place else to go. You tell me who was out there, baby.
Those people knew how to demonstrate. They'd been
around. They came out with all their riot gear. They
had done it before. This is not your "weekend demonstrators." Those people were up there fighting for you
and me. Those people had been gassed before. They had
been maced before. They'd been thrown in jail before.
They'd been beaten up before. And they did it for you.
Don't you sit over there and tell me how they got in
their Jaguars and went back to Columbia!

RESPONDER (black): They even help us compose our songs!
All right. They were doing this for you and me, but
what changed them? Have they changed?

MR. RUDD: Socialism hasn't occurred yet. The revolution is not here yet. That takes time.

RESPONDER (black): They can stand there beside us and get beat up every night, but don't tell me they're my allies. I look around. I don't see them here. Where are they now? Are they still in Grant Park, taking up those so-called issues they were standing up for? Are they still there? Where are they?

MR. RUDD: There aren't many real revolutionaries in the country, and I don't consider myself to be one. But on the other hand, there are people who are trying everywhere they are to develop this movement and to fight. Look what happened out at San Francisco State. At State there are some black demands, and you had thousands of kids go out on strike.

RESPONDER (black): Look what happened downtown in Atlanta for King's memorial vigil where all of our white brothers were out there playing their Rolling Stones or whatever the group is; laying up there in their air mattresses!

MR. RUDD: Oh, come on! We don't have to say who has the most balls or anything! Where were you? That's ridiculous. We can't put this on a one-to-one level. There are revolutionary organizations in the white. But I believe they are beginning. That's all I'm talking about.

QUESTIONER: Who is the general in this revolution?

MR. RUDD: There is none. I'll give you an example to follow in your direction: the Berkeley strike. I was out in San Francisco one month ago. The Third World Liberation Front controls that strike a hundred per-cent, top to bottom, and there's nobody else who has a word to say. I talked to kids out there on strike who said, "We don't like what they're doing, but we're on strike with those people, and they're in charge." I've gone up to those kids and said, "What the hell are you doing over there?" And they say, "TWLF is running the strike."

RESPONDER (black): This is precisely what I'm saying.
Perhaps strike and the closing of the schools is not in
our best interest, but you seem to think it is, and
therefore you have the strikes and you close the schools.

MR. RUDD: They're led by black people.

RESPONDER (black): We know in many ways how black
people are led through white people infiltrating.

RESPONDER (white): Just perhaps as a point of fact,
during the latter part of his life, one of the things
that Malcolm X regretted the most was the time when he
was still with the Black Muslims and a white girl came
into a Muslim restaurant and asked him with tears in her
eyes what she could do to help, and he said, "Nothing."

RESPONDER (black): Many of us are here; all of us have
different opinions. I want to express my appreciation
for Mark's answers. I appreciated your building this
case for revolt. I sat here listening, and I heard you
say some of the same things that I've said! I'll tell
you one thing you're doing, one thing we all need and
that is, to know who the enemy is. I can't relate my
long hair to your long.hair because it doesn't look the
same way, but I can relate to your honesty; I can relate
to your humanness. I think that what you're driving at
is that you want to be honest with yourself. When you
really find something you want to do in life, you must
be ready to die for it. I have promised myself I can
die for it. You promised yourself you could die for it.

When we find the enemy, he's going to be the oppressor, regardless of whether he's black or white. I
had a friend who was robbed just a few days ago by the
brothers. He said, "The brothers did it and that's all
right." But actually that doesn't help. It doesn't
help because the guy had an Afro and big lips. I'm

looking for that oppressor. I don't care who he is. If he oppresses me then I'm against him. That's who I'll shoot, that's who I'm against.

I think petty arguments are something that keep us from getting down to the nitty gritty. What we need to do is just be honest in what we're driving at. There's one common enemy. We all have it.

QUESTIONER: You mentioned the fact earlier that you were born into the Jewish religion, am I to understand that you are no longer a Jew?

MR. RUDD: Yes.

QUESTIONER: Do you see Christianity or, perhaps, Judaism in some form tied up in this entire imperialistic, racist thing that the United States is doing? Do you think that people go along with the Christianity as just another psych to make imperialism look legitimate?

RESPONDER: Let *me* answer that question! Any power structure can be used to dehumanize and oppose and oppress people. I don't care what it is. It can be the church. If any structure gets enough power that it doesn't have to answer to us, it can oppress us.

MR. RUDD: I think your question about religion being an oppressor is important. Christianity talks about salvation, not in this world but in some better world. There's a lot of passivity involved in such an ideology.

THE BLACK AS A COLONIZED MAN[*]

Shirley Chisholm

Today, all over this country, there is confusion reigning, as we black people try at long last to find our rightful place in American society. Before we are able to find our rightful place, there are many things that we are going to have to face realistically. I think it is very important that we go back a bit and see ourselves in total perspective from the days of slavery right up to now. And so tonight, I choose to address you on "The Black As A Colonized Man."

There is little doubt that in some ways the black American is a colonized man. One needs only to point to the ghetto as proof of one aspect of his colonization. However, colonization is more than living together in the same area. Since the situation of the black American, past and present, differs so radically from that of other colonized people, I would like to examine it in some depth.

There are two basic groups of colonized people: immigrants who migrate to a country, and natives of a country which some other more powerful country captures. Black Americans, it is obvious, fit into neither one of these two categories. The immigrant usually leaves his homeland by choice. There may be many factors such as

---

133

religious, economic, social, or political persecution
that influence him, but it is generally true that he
is looking for a better way of life. If he has somehow
acquired the necessary social and cultural tools, or if
his own culture is not too divergent from that of the
host country, he may be able to move directly into at
least the economic midstream. If he doesn't have the
requisite tools, knowledge of the host language, some
needed or desirable labor skills, and at least a rudi-
mentary education, he must find some way to acquire them
and to survive at the same time. What one does then,
of course, is to seek out people like himself, often a
sister, a brother or a friend for help, advice and security. Even more often he does this before leaving
his home country. Eventually this process creates a
colony from which individuals filter out slowly into
the host society. And often these colonies are simply
called neighborhoods - the Italian neighborhood, the
Jewish neighborhood, and so on.

The situation for the black American differed in
that (1) he was transported largely against his will,
(2) his own culture was intentionally obliterated and
destroyed, (3) the skills that he had were of relatively
little use to the host country, (4) his own language
was destroyed for the most part by deliberately sep-
arating him from his fellow tribesmen, and the language
that was used by the slave masters to communicate with
him emanated from the whip and the club, (5) his family
and his social ties were deliberately broken, (6) there
was no way in which he could build, or marshal political
power. There, of course, are other differences, but
these six constituted the major ones.

In the case of the colonial natives, persons who
owned and occupied the land before the interloper, the
colonist forced his way in. Such a situation also differed significantly from that of the first black Americans. Guns and clubs were only moderately successful
in destroying the culture of the colonial native even

though they served to keep him docile. The native had
in that respect the same advantage that the immigrant
had over the first slaves. He could maintain his
language, his family structure, village or tribal ties,
his religion and other basic elements of his culture.
Because he could retain the transmittance of his culture, he was free to perpetuate at least a fascimile
of his formal life style. But, for the newly arrived
slave, there was the future of deliberate and constant
breaking of cultural ties that I have mentioned.

Even more important was the fact that the major
ingredients of his life style were the force and violence perpetrated upon him. From dawn to dawn, twenty-
four hours a day, these were the driving force of his
life and were used by the slave masters to accomplish
the governing of every aspect of his life, whether it
was planting, harvesting or breeding. I know that much
of this is already known to many of you in this audience,
but I think that it is very necessary for me to repeat
it in order to make a very crucial point. In general
terms, the slave can be said to have existed in a cultural limbo. He had nothing.

There were a few exceptions. There existed some
vestiges of various African crafts such as weaving, wood-
working and ironworking. Drums were used for communication and music, work songs, and spirituals showed
African influence. And because it was virtually impossible to separate people from the same tribes completely,
there were vestiges of the African languages left. The
other major exceptions were the "house Negroes" and the
relatively few freedmen. Both of these groups had already begun the process that E. Franklin Frazier eu-
phemistically calls "acculturation."*

---

* RACE AND CULTURE CONTACTS IN THE MODERN WORLD con-
tains one of Frazier's discussions of acculturation,
emphasizing that the process was different for the

The fact that the vast majority of black slaves
lived in a cultural void is one of the prime reasons
that the situation of black Americans even today should
not be seen as strictly analogous to colonialism. The
colonized native can choose between retaining his old
culture or accepting the colonialist, or as in the case
of the immigrant, the host culture. But, for the black
slave, there existed a void not only culturally but
politically and also economically. It was the political and the economic void that was to prove most damaging to him.

The end of the Civil War freed some four million
slaves. And it was at this point that black Americans
in mass were faced with the most crucial decision -
accept return to an Africa that most had never seen,
accept the life styles and cultural norms of the dominant society, or somehow build a new life and culture
base from scratch. I use the word "decision" because
in retrospect it would seem to have been a decision,
but in truth the die was already cast. The freedmen,
North and South, had already set their feet upon a path.
The uneducated, almost decultured, black masses had no
choice but to follow. There was nothing to do but to
accept that dominant western culture.

---

various elements in the black, enslaved populations.
The author claims that "the mixed blood was more likely
to have intimate contacts with Europeans, which would
facilitate his acquisition of European culture ... (and)
in the United States it was generally the son of a mu-
latto household servant who was apprenticed to learn
some skilled trade." Frazier acknowledges that "this
does not mean that the plantation has been the only
means by which the colored peoples of the modern world
have acquired European culture, but it was an elementary
form of social organization which played the most important role in the first stages of acculturation."
(p. 246)

Before I go further, there are two factors that
will be essential to establish. The first has to do
with the different situations of the colonial native
and the immigrant particularly in a capitalistic country. Franz Fanon in *The Wretched of the Earth* gives
excellent insight into the motivating factors of both
the colonial and capitalistic worlds. He points out
that for the native in the colonial world the dividing
line, the frontier, is clearly delineated by the bar-
racks and the police station. The intermediaries
between the powerful and the powerless are the soldiers
and the police. He counterposes against this system
of open force and brutality the capitalistic system
of using education, and I put that word "education" in
quotes. The passed-on structure of moral reflexes, the
gold watch or medal at the end of the long and faith-
ful service, and other aesthetic expressions are designed to lighten the task of policing what the exploiter must perform.* It is important to remember that
the black American has always lived in a capitalistic
democracy that has not hesitated to use violence as well
as "education".

---

*For Fanon, the enslavement through "education" may
occur even after a colonizer has been rejected by newly-
independent nations and peoples. For the national middle-class often quickly acts out the roles previously
assumed by foreign exploiters. "The middle class dis-
covers its historic mission: that of intermediary.
Seen through its eyes, its mission has nothing to do
with transforming the nation; it consists, prosaically,
of being the transmission line between the nation and
a capitalism, rampant though camouflaged, which today
puts on the mask of neo-colonialism." (p. 152 ff., THE
WRETCHED OF THE EARTH). An interpretation of national-
ization which actually contradicts national interests
becomes a basis of middle-class reaction and, according
to Fanon, the means by which previous unfair advantage
is simply transferred to national class interests.

A second factor that is essential to establish at
this point is the political and social context of the
south at the end of the Civil War. It was then, I feel,
that the black American began to become colonized. The
nation and particularly the south was in tumultuous
disorder politically, socially and economically. The
country had fought a war based primarily on economics
that the north had only disguised as a war for social
justice. Even the President had said that the most important factor was the non-dissolution of the union.
The country, north and south, found itself with two
problems it was ill-prepared to solve. The abolishment
of slavery had been accomplished, but the nation was
still split asunder. And a second problem, of course,
was what to do with four million freed Negroes. Dr.
Rayford Logan* described the situation thus:

> "Quite apart from consideration of
> race and class, the elements of a
> community that have long exercised
> exclusive control of government do
> not generally relinquish that con-
> trol without a struggle."

The contest in the south, however, was initially

---

*   Rayford W. Logan, a black historian who taught at
Atlanta University from 1933 until 1938, wrote several
volumes on the diplomatic relationships between black
and non-black nations. See his OPERATION OF THE MAN-
DATE SYSTEM IN AFRICA. He also edited the early study
of southern mass media entitled THE ATTITUDE OF THE
SOUTHERN WHITE PRESS TOWARD NEGRO SUFFRAGE, 1932-1940.
For a shorter analysis of his views on the black struggle in America see his chapter, "The Negro Wants First-
Class Citizenship" in WHAT THE NEGRO WANTS (University
of North Carolina Press: Chapel Hill).

embittered by the difference in race and culture. Therefore, the years immediately following the Civil War were
perilous and trying ones for the southern black.   Most
white southerners either participated in or condoned the
political frauds that brought home rule back to Tennessee, for example, as early as 1869 and to three more
states the next year.   And many white southerners also
either condoned or participated in the intimidation by
violence and terror as exemplified by the Ku Klux Klan
and similar groups.   Some of the most significant advances in many southern state constitutions were accomplished in that period, but in most cases, as soon
as home rule returned they were either wiped out or
replaced by the infamous black codes.   In fact, throughout that entire period everything that looked as if it
might benefit black folks was systematically destroyed
either by law or by violence.   Unfortunately, it was
at this point that education or, more to the point, the
lack of education had its greatest impact upon the new
black American.

     Education has always had as its primary task im-
parting not only the history of a culture but, in fact,
the transmission of the culture itself.   For Franz Fanon's
colonial native or for the immigrant, education was a
process of cultural superimposition at best or cultural
transplantation by choice and design at the worst.   Education for the freed slave was cultural implantation.
He had no choice.   What I am saying is this: in order
to continue to exist to do simple daily things like
feeding one's family, if one had a family, the freedman
had to begin to submit to the cultural norms of those
who seemed superior to him.   In short, to make it in
"Charley's world" he had to imitate "Charley."

     At least three white groups who were in the south
were aware of the impact that education for the masses
of blacks would have on their own conceptions and goals
for a future society.   They were the northern white

liberals, the southern white conservatives, and the
southern moderates. For northern liberals, education
for the Negro was the way toward an entirely new social
order and they, as Horace Mann Bond stated it, "wished
to use the schools for the Negroes as the instrument
for leveling all vestiges of the past."[*] For the southern conservative, education for blacks meant potential
black political and economic power. These were two
factors that would be fatal to their goal of a new south,
constructed from the patterns of and shaped in the mode
of the old south. The white southern moderate saw education of black people in what was perhaps the clearest
context: a method or a means of continuing control of
the lives of black people.

Those groups of southern whites saw the danger of
allowing the northern white liberal to educate black
people. The northern liberals, composed mainly of
abolitionists, church groups, and missionary societies
were not just idle dreamers. Barely six months into
the Civil War, the American Missionary Society established a day school for what the Union commander of the
area called "contraband of war" at Fortress Monroe,
Virginia. That school still exists. Today it is Hampton Institute. Hampton set the tone for the rest of
the American black schools, especially those established
by the liberals.[**] The schools were intended to impart

_____

[*]From THE EDUCATION OF THE NEGRO IN THE AMERICAN
SOCIAL ORDER, chapter II, "Social Classes and the Beginning of Reconstruction." This definitive study of
black academic institutions was originally published in
1934 and reprinted with an additional chapter, "A 1965
Retrospective of American Negro Education", in 1966.
Horace Mann Bond, former professor at Atlanta University,
is the father of State Representative Julian Bond.

[**]As Mrs. Chisholm notes, Hampton became the prototype for black higher education along with Tuskegee In-

thrift, piety and industry primarily, and they did. It
must be remembered that the schools were operated and
controlled for a number of years by the same people who
were setting up and running missionary schools throughout the world. It must also be remembered that thrift,
piety, and industry were the cardinal virtues of the
religio-ethical background of the majority of these
founders. (I don't mean to disparage the work of those
good people, but a few things must be pointed out if we
are to understand where we are and where we are going!)
First, what they were doing was imposing a culture upon
black people. Second, they didn't fully comprehend the
political and the social context in which they found
themselves. They were "educational carpetbaggers."
They had, though, a very impressive saving grace. They
believed and helped demonstrate on a significant scale
that black people could be educated and this factor had
telling force, particularly upon black people themselves.
There was one other major factor involved as far as
southern education was concerned - the Bureau of Freedmen. It is important to note the presence of the Bureau
for two reasons: (1) it was involved in establishing

------

stitute which was founded by a distinguished Hampton
graduate, Booker T. Washington. General Samuel Chapman
Armstrong was a major influence in determining the industrial character of Hampton's educational policies;
he had observed the program at the Labor School in Hilo,
Hawai and became convinced "mechanical labor" could be
correlated with moral strength in newly-freed black
communities. As Franklin Frazier says in BLACK BOUR-
GEOISIE, "Although the majority of the schools established by the Bureau and religious organizations were
called 'colleges' and 'universities', most of their
instruction did not go beyond a secondary level and only
one institution, Howard University, ever became (during
the twentieth century) a real university with the various
professional schools." (p. 59)

and sustaining a number of schools, and (2) the charges
of graft and corruption that hung over it provided further fuel to feed the southern whites' anger. Southern
opposition to education for black people then took many
forms, not the least of which were school burnings,
teacher beatings and the siphoning off of funds intended
for Negro schools. Another formidable and effective
weapon was the smear campaign instituted by whites.
They claimed that the Negro child wasn't worth educat-
ing, that he couldn't or he wouldn't learn. They
claimed that the moral standards of the Yankee school
"marms" left a great deal to be desired. Some of this may
seem irrelevant. It isn't! The job of making the black
American a colonized man and a "cultured neo-native"
had only begun. Education was to finish the task. And
these were the forces that shaped education for the black
man in the south.

A strange unholy alliance took place in the period
that followed Reconstruction. It was left to the southern moderates, black and white, to cast down their buck-
ets and make the best of what had become an intolerable
situation for both. As I indicated earlier, the white
moderates realized that the brand of education dispensed
by northern white liberals spelled absolute doom for the
hope of salvaging anything at all of the pre-war southern life style. And most of them also recognized the
fact that some form of education was inevitable. So,
these two factors combined to give them impetus to do
two things. First, they involved themselves in maintaining schools for blacks, often at private expense.
Second, they moved to control public education of black
students.

Black leaders also realized the absolute need of
education for the masses of black people. They were
also extremely aware of the political and the social
context in which they existed. No one can say for sure
whether those early Negro schools and educators would
have survived at all if they had become embroiled in

the political and social holocaust that was raging in
the south. Therefore, no one can say that blacks were
completely wrong in their choice of curriculum and direction. We do know, though, some of the results of
that emphasis on industrial education. W.E.B. DuBois
has pointed out that such an emphasis would mean that
Negroes would no longer demand a right to the same public education as whites, or integration. He said that
such an education was intended to make black students
docile and servile.

There are other factors, but as I look back over
what has happened to us in this country I believe that
DuBois was right. The majority of graduates from Negro
schools went into teaching in other southern Negro
schools, carrying with them the colonized attitude and
spreading it. I cannot say that they were wrong, just
as I cannot say that the schools were wrong. In many
ways, the schools and the teachers of that day, in that
time, and in that place, were as militant and courageous
as were the students and civil rights workers of the
1950's and the 1960's. But, it must be said that the
type of education available on the one hand and the lack
of education for many on the other produced a break
between the classes of black people that made it easy
to maintain control or colonization, if you will, of all
black people. I have taken this time to tell you what
Malcolm X summed up in one brief paragraph! And this
is what he said:

> "The slave master took Tom and
> dressed him well, fed him well
> and even gave him a little edu-
> cation, a *little* education.
> Gave him a long coat and a top
> hat and made all the other
> slaves look up to him. Then he
> used Tom to control them."*

---

*Malcolm's description of the white man's use and

Some of you look a little uneasy! But let me say
to you, if ever we are going to one day become a race
of unconquerable men and unconquerable women, we have
got to face the truth! The reason that I took so much
time to develop that thesis is to show you that there
were extenuating circumstances in those days. I must
remind you that there are very few of those kinds of
circumstances today. We no longer have good reason to
perpetrate or succumb to innocuous minds in order to
get education. These "minds" are dying to control you!

Students today want to know about power, especially
economic and political power. Everybody wants to know
about power; why not us? And that is true whatever we
are studying. Black educators, north and south, are
going to have to involve themselves in these areas.
Particularly in the south is this important. Almost 80
percent of the black students who received B.A.'s last
year were graduated by southern schools that were predominantly black. Just as important to the southern
schools and, therefore, presumably to all black Americans
is the financial crisis that these schools are facing.
In order to overcome it, those who run the schools,
those who attend the schools, and those who support them

---

misuse of blacks is found throughout his AUTOBIOGRAPHY
and, in its early chapters, he recalls his first en-
counters with the deception. He writes, "I don't care
how nice one (white) is to you; the thing you must remember is that almost never does he really see you as
he sees himself, as he sees his own kind. He may stand
with you through thin, but not thick ... it has historically been the case with white people, in their regard
for black people, that even though we might be with them,
we weren't considered of them." (p. 27) George Breitman's
thesis in THE LAST YEAR OF MALCOLM X is that Malcolm
modified this stance after contact with Algerian and
other light-skinned revolutionaries during his trips to
Africa in 1964.

are going to have to become manageable in economics and
in politics very quickly. The education that you will
receive in trying to save your lives as institutions
will have to be transferred to your students as soon as
you can possibly do it. Students want to know about
power. They want that power to make some important
changes. Changes not only in the colonial status of
black Americans but in the fabric of the country itself.
It would behoove us to give them access to that knowledge for two reasons: one, it is their birthright and
two, they intend to try to make those changes with or
without sophisticated knowledge!

     Educational leaders of today must involve them-
selves in the life of the communities that swirl around
them. We have to understand the reason for upheaval
in this country. We have to recognize that we are going
through a very real social revolution: black people
revolting, students revolting, and even women revolting
in some parts of the nation. Any society that has so
many segments simultaneously revolting requires its
members to stop and ask why.

     We like to find a scapegoat, and many of us blame
the student. We say, "Look at what's happened to
students!" But, the students of this country, black
and/or white, didn't develop in a vacuum. They didn't
drop out of the air and land here! They're the products
of a society that has practiced sham and hypocrisy.
Products of a society where the leadership in both the
public and the private sectors has said, "Do as I say;
not as I act."

     I certainly don't condone all of the actions
students are indulging in. But, I understand why they
are indulging! Some of the older folk just don't want
to "tune in." Those who have been the beneficiaries
of the status quo, both black and white, are not about
to let anybody in. But we've got to understand that
since we're speaking about the concept of brotherhood,

of giving every individual the right to develop his full-
est potential, we're going to have to make changes.
Change is in the nature of things in a constantly moving,
automated, and technological society.

Black people are saying that we're through with
tokenism, we're through with gradualism, and we're
through with "see-how-far-you've-comeism." On the other
hand, students are saying we are through with sham and
hypocrisy. It behooves those of us who recognize that
our society is deteriorating to get out of our complacent,
satisfied selfs and accept the challenge, provide the
kind of imagery that our young people can respect. I've
been on thirty-five campuses in twenty-two different
states in the past nine months, and I can tell you one
thing: thank God for the young people! If nothing else,
the young people in this country have a deeper sense of
commitment to cultural justice which would make America
what it should become. If we don't provide the kind of
courageous leadership that students can accept, they
are not going to ask for anything. They're going to
"do their own thing."

I've been very glad to have had the opportunity to
bring to you my thoughts on the black as a colonized
man. I come to you as a person who has spent seventeen
years in the educational arena, and four years in the
New York State Legislature and, now, the United States
Congress. I have experienced years of involvement in
my community before I emerged politically five years ago.
I speak to you out of the depth of my own experiences.
And, I want to leave you tonight with this: the time
has come when we black people shall no longer be the
passive recipients of whatever the morals or the politics
of a nation may decree for us. We shall rise up and
speak out, take a stand, have guts, have courage and
look only to God and to our consciences for approval!

DIALOGUE WITH MRS. CHISHOLM

QUESTIONER: Does the election of the Nixon Administration mean repression for black people?

MRS. CHISHOLM: The Nixon Administration thus far, if
one can judge it by its actions, is an era of retro-
gression of the worst kind. We are moving back on every
level. Take anything: social legislation, educational
legislation, the priorities of the nation, even the
appointments that are made. In spite of the fact, for
example, that not only black America but white America
was saying something negative about this man called
"Haynesworth," President Nixon said he was still going
to push the nomination. Now what can you say? What is
happening in America? It forebodes ill for us. That's
all I can say right now, and I'm there every day in
Washington watching what's happening. The picture does
not look good at all for us.

QUESTIONER: What's your solution?

MRS. CHISHOLM: Let me put it to you in a practical,
pragmatic sense. We're fourteen or fifteen percent
of the population of this country. We have no economic
power. We have no real political power, although we
are beginning to develop it particularly in the south
of the country in contrast to the north. A people who
do not have economic power in a capitalistic society
find it very difficult to move. One thing we as a
people have not learned yet which we've got to learn is
that we must unify. It's all right to go around and
sit-in and lie-in, and sit-out and lie-out, and say that
the man has his foot on our necks, and "Mr. Charley" did
me this and he did me that. But do you know what they
said - when I was in the New York legislature and even
in Washington, D.C.? If the day should ever come that
the black people would get together, America would really
change! Parenthetically, they know that we're not going
to get together.

Now, brother, you don't have to like me or I don't
have to like you, but the fact of the matter is we're
bound together by a commonality and that commonality is
our skin pigmentation. Even though you may see things
a little differently from me, man, you and I look alike;
which means, if you understand what power is, we must
do as other ethnic groups have done in this country.
They came to these shores and got together around certain common things that were necessary for their survival as a group. Today as we look at some organizations, we can still tell by their names whether they
are Jewish or Italian or Irish. When these people came
from Europe, hardly able to speak the English language,
man, they learned it here. They acquired a certain
know-how and economic and/or educational power.

What's the next thing that most people want when
they have money and education? They want political
power. So, in New York City you had different groups
fighting each other for such power. The Sicilians even
fought against the Neopolitans, but later came together
in New York City to get power; after all, they are all
Italians! We've got to do it. We've got to come together. And the moment that we come together we can
help change our destiny in these United States of
America.

I don't care what your philosophy is. We've all
had different experiences. We've all been exposed to
different stimuli. I can't expect to think exactly like
you or you to think like me, man. But the fact of the
matter is that if we're talking about power to control
our destiny, we must cease being petty and get together.
The moment we get together we will overcome everything.

QUESTIONER: What is your solution to black politicians
who don't identify with their people?

MRS. CHISHOLM: My solution is quite simple. (I'll probably get in trouble again!) I feel the time has come
when no political party in this country should have black

people in its pocket. If the Republican party wants
our vote and/or if the Democratic party wants our vote,
we should be in such a psychological frame of mind
that our behavior in terms of our voting patterns would
make them put up candidates of a kind that would bid for
our votes. But nobody has to bid for our votes. When
we go into the booth to vote, we go right down the line.
We don't even ask anything about some of the candidates.
We've got to become selective in terms of black candidates because, we aren't that great in number. The few
black officials that we have to fight, fight, fight.

I'm a Democrat, or supposed to be! I'm a national
committeewoman for the Democratic Party in the State of
New York and, honey, the bosses didn't put me in that
spot; you better believe me! The moment that I came
out for John Lindsay everybody became upset. Why should
they become upset? They became upset, because I happen
to be one of the high-ranking Democratic politicians in
this country today, and I would probably influence quite
a number of black voters. That's wrong. Don't you know
that the Democratic party in New York City can always
depend on blacks and could always put anything up?

Let's stop giving people our votes; let's get rid
of those black politicians who don't answer our needs.
We have no more time for a couple of bosses, black bosses
and/or white bosses, getting into a back room and deciding which candidates are best for us, the people.
We've got to put an end to that. I'm sorry if there are
some good Democrats here or if there are some good Republicans, but this is the truth. The truth shall set
you free!

QUESTIONER: Don't you feel that black as well as white
politicians are compelled to follow the folkways and
mores of success?

MRS. CHISHOLM: People say to me, "Shirley, you speak
out on so many things. You are always embroiled in

controversies. You don't act like a politician. There
are some things you should not do which are not politically expedient to do." I tell them it is important for
me to operate so that my people have faith and trust in
me. I have a very good education; I can always make at
least "ten," at *least* ten! I don't want to be rich.
Therefore, it has to be a philosophy, a commitment with
me.

Why should one expect a black politician to be any
different from a white politician? Why do we want to
set up different standards for the black politician? I
don't really want to, but the circumstances of life are
such in American society that we will not have the per-
centage of politicians to represent us on the basis of
our population. So, those few that we have must make a
commitment to our people; they must go beyond political
expediency.

People say you can't be effective legislatively if
you continue to keep rocking the boat. Well, let me
tell you something! When I served in the New York State
Legislature, the Speaker of the House used to say to me,
"I don't understand you, Shirley, because you have just
as many Republicans as Democrats voting for your bills."
Do you know why? It's not what you do, it's how you do
it. They may not always have agreed with my philosophy
in the New York State Legislature, but they knew I was
not hypocritical, and that my actions through the years
have indicated this. Somebody who might have been reluctant to give me a vote would say, "She fights, she
fights so hard, she's for real. We'll give her the vote!"
I passed nine bills and had them signed into law, a record for a black freshman in New York State. And yet, I
was called a maverick, and the second day that I went
to the Legislature they told me I was committing political suicide. Now, four years later, I'm in the United
States Congress. If committing political suicide can
cause my meteoric rise in four years, I love committing
political suicide!

QUESTIONER: How can the black community control its educational destiny?

MRS. CHISHOLM: Most of you have been reading a great deal about the Oceanhill-Brownsville situation. That was the beginning of the first, real black fight for community control of education. Parents had been noticing inequities in New York for quite some time, and statistics were indicating that the children of the ghetto and/or so-called "socially deprived" areas were below in math levels, reading levels, every kind of level. These parents already had two and three sons or daughters in their families who couldn't read or couldn't cope in this automated society. They became very interested in controlling their schools by taking over their local school boards themselves. I don't have to go through the whole story, but I want to give you a perspective.

The New York State Legislature didn't want to institute community control. They felt that if black people began to control their schools this would encourage efforts for further controls. Although that was not played up a great deal in the papers, this was at the root of it. But the people were determined even if it were not done through legal means or legislative means. And so the bill was passed. It was a watered-down bill, but it was a beginning of some semblance of community control. In New York City today you find school districts that are still fighting; you find others that have accepted that moderate-type control bill; and the educational battle is raging.

New York State gets twenty-one thousand regent scholarships every year; *twenty-one thousand!* In Brooklyn, in my district, one year we had two regent scholarhips, another year four, another year one. Why? Is it because black kids are inherently dumb? No, it's because of the kind of educational curriculum that these kinds have had to undergo. When it came time to take

all kinds of scholastic achievement and aptitude tests,
they just couldn't compete. The regent scholarships,
naturally, went to those who were prepared. This is
the battle that is raging in New York City. I predict
that we are going to succeed, because some of us are
committed to making this thing work.

QUESTIONER: Do you not feel that bussing corrects some
educational inequities?

MRS. CHISHOLM: At one time, and I'll be very honest
with you, I was a strong advocate of bussing. I'll
tell you why. I used to see how these regent scholarships would go to white students, and black and Puerto
Rican kids just couldn't get a scholarship or they
couldn't sit for one because of the kind of education
they were getting. I said, maybe we'd better trans-
port them if transporting means they would have good
educational facilities and the kind of curriculum that
would enable them to compete. But then, two things
hit me. First, we were transporting a certain
number of black kids and leaving the bulk behind
every day in the community. Second, I saw psychological damage to black kids; I saw them have to get
psychological and psychiatric attention because the
white community was not ready to receive them, and those
kids were too young to cope with what was being done to
them there. I saw black kids six and seven years old
damaged. This went to me; I don't think there's anything, *anything* that should damage a child whether he's
black or white. I wondered what are we doing?

Until we can do something about the housing patterns of these United States, the schools are going to
reflect a particular neighborhood. Since the bulk of
black children still has to live in certain neighborhoods, we are going to focus our energies now on lifting
up these schools, on the curriculum in these schools,
on the kinds of teachers we have in these schools. We

are going to fight for community control because the
masses, the bulk of black children, have to stay in a
particular community. We must make the schools acceptable so that these black children will be able to go
out and cope with other children on their level. Once
they have that training, one can integrate afterward.

My premise is this: I'm always concerned with what
will happen to the majority in a situation, not the
privileged few. I used to see in a particular area in
Brooklyn two busses every morning taking eighty black
and Puerto Rican kids out of the neighborhood. Then
I would see all the other black kids who were left to
go to our dilapidated schools. I said, "no." I began
to reverse and center my fight on the schools themselves. If a parent wants to bus a child and can do
so, all right. But I am talking about the welfare
mother. I am talking about the masses whose children
will still be left behind in that bussing system. We
must make our neighborhood system prepare those kids
for the future.

QUESTIONER: What do you think about the black community's attempt to identify with African culture?

MRS. CHISHOLM: Years ago, nobody wanted to be identified as an African. All of a sudden there is this terrific identification attempt. This is good. We are
beginning to assert ourselves, and we are beginning to
feel very proud of our heritage. But on the other hand,
it is not enough to acquire the trappings of this heritage. Many Africans have said to me, "Mrs. Chisholm,
we come here and find the black Americans acquiring our
trappings, our garb and what have you, and we're glad
to see it. Years ago they didn't want to bother with
us. But we want them to sit down with us and plan what
is going to be done in terms of blacks here and over
there; what is going to be the common thread that we
can weave together so that the world will have to respect all black men." Unfortunately, they have found
in some instances that there isn't a lot of substance

to the movement here in America. They've been discour-
aged as they found that beneath the veneer people haven't
really wanted to be serious about the black movement.

I happen to feel that if we can find this common
thread, that if we can identify and establish certain
common goals, we will become powerful, not only in America but also abroad. But it's going to have to be more
than just superficialities. We're going to have to
travel to Africa, sit down in their capitals and in
their homes, and work out plans and goals for the black
people of the world. This must replace the present
little social shindigs where you meet Africans of different backgrounds and, when you come back, you tell
your friends: "Oh man, I went here and I can settle for
it!" This means nothing. The substance in terms of
goals and power, I think, must come.

QUESTIONER: How would you relate the term "black power"
to the problem of economic power?

MRS. CHISHOLM: My definition of black power might be
different from many people's. Every group has achieved
some kind of power, but when other groups achieved it
you didn't have to use any adjective before the noun
"power": it was known that it was going to be white
power. Black power today is merely the consolidation
of the rages and the reactions of the black people in
America because of the failure of the white majority to
respond to their aspirations and their hopes. That's
all black power is.

We need economic power, but in setting it we've
got to look at our priorities. What do I mean by that?
(We have some wealthy black people in America, but you
should see what they are concerned with!) We're going
to have to put our dollars and the brain power that we
have, both as professional and businessmen, and begin
to create empires, little economic empires. We must
show the brother that those of us who have had the op-

portunity to receive a business and a professional education know how to put it to relevant and meaningful
use.

I'm going to step on some of your toes now! I saw
something recently about which I almost puked! This
black brother rented a silver slipper to put on his dance
table at fifty dollars for the evening. You know what
that slipper did? (It's beautiful, you know!) You pour
the champagne in it, and it comes through the tip of the
toe and into the glasses. Yet when they went around to
the brother to try to get money for scholarships - "No."
Priorities, man, priorities!

We are so brainwashed. We have been so used to
aping and imitating we don't seem to recognize that if
we are going to move out, and if we want to look at
"the man" eyeball to eyeball, we're going to have to
come up in the economic structure. There's no reason
why black people in many of the communities across this
country that have money can't get together and establish
cooperatives and factories. I know seven places right
now where you could get together at least seven hundred
thousand dollars in each of these communities. But
what do they do? They sit back and they buy additional
mink, an additional "Caddy," and then they talk about
how we're going to get there. We've got to look at our
priorities. We've got to change our life style a little
bit. We've got to realize that we can't wear three and
four minks at the same time.

You see, it's just as bad to replace one kind of
master for another kind. I don't care what his color
is. We must mean that we want to see our people move
out and up, and if we are in a position to make this
contribution we need to "get up off of it." Then we
begin to show by example. We can't go around blaming
the man for everything. Really folks, please, we've got
to take a good look at ourselves, too, and see what it
is that we are not doing to help to move our own people
along.

QUESTIONER: Will part of the present war budget be
allocated for domestic social needs if or when the
United States withdraws from Vietnam?

MRS. CHISHOLM: Nobody in the administration has indicated that when the war in Vietnam ends that money is
going to be appropriated to take care of the domestic
war that's going on here, that is, the war in the cities.
Nobody has said that. They make sure that they do not
put out those press statements. The people of America
should become watchdogs as to where this 80 percent of
the budget that has been spent for the military for this
war is going to be allocated because, honey, you already
have the lobbyist groups of all kinds just waiting to
get their percentages. I can tell you, with the mood
and the direction of this administration, and the fact
that President Nixon has to pay back a tremendous political debt, it ain't about to come to us! This is
something that we're going to have to watch, prepare
ourselves for, and almost launch a monumental assault
upon when this war is over. The war might end sooner
than we expect. We don't know. The questions that you
should be asking yourselves are: where is the money
going; and, what will we do if the money doesn't come
to help our segment of American society become a part
of the so-called "American Dream."

QUESTIONER: Do the words "black power" reflect the
essence of black revolution?

MRS. CHISHOLM: I think that in every revolution there
is always the coinage of certain phrases which catch the
imagination in terms of the direction in which that revolution must move. In order to have adherence, it is
very necessary to have the kinds of phrases and programs
and slogans that will dramatize that which you are
seeking. The term "black power," like other terms existing, is a characteristic of this revolution that we're
going through. Many of us don't become upset by the
term, because we understand the context in which it developed and why black people use it.

You see, it is the word "black" that bothers people,
I think. For a long time we've had all kinds of power
in this country but, as I said earlier, we never used
the adjective "white" because we had been relegated to a
subservient status, and we had stayed in our places nice-
ly over the years. We didn't worry about whether we
were going to fight for power; we assumed that power was
going to be white power.

All we are saying in this revolution is that we,
too, have learned what every other ethnic group has
learned and has put into action. Lest anybody mistakes
what it's all about, we're not going to take anymore to
tokenism, and we are going to put the word "black" before the word "power"!   We shall overcome that phrase,
"black power." But when we do, we'll remember that
"black power" also came along!

ONLY IN A NEW AMERICA

Harry Golden

I don't have the advantage of speakers who speak
on a set subject like Vietnam or how I write books. I
have been to Provo, Utah, to speak at Brigham Young, a
Mormon College; the next night to Loyola University,
Roman Catholic, and then the Methodist Board of Social
Action; then the next night the NAACP and the Bonds for
Israel; and you can't tell all of these people the same
thing. But, all these speeches begin with a dinner.
This is something the Jews invented: "No eating, no
meeting." While the Anglo Saxons were still roaming the
forests of Great Britain painting their bodies blue and
eating wild berries, we Jews already had diabetes! A
young man said, "Americans are interested in three things,"
not necessarily in the order in which I place them, "communism, calories and body odor."

They've asked me at the universities how I am able
to thrive in the South with Chambers of Commerce giving
me dinners and the university giving me a "Harry Golden
Day". I told them it is because I put a little humor
in my writings. If Galileo had used a bit of humor when
he presented his ideas not even the Inquisition would
have touched him. The Golden Vertical Plan, for example,
is something that people in the deep South couldn't

159

afford not to print.*

I will never forget a fellow came to see me, called me at 10:00 o'clock that night from the bus station, and I said, "It's pretty late." He was from the American Friends Service Committee, and it didn't enter my mind that he might be a Negro or not. I said, "I will get you a room at the Hotel Charlotte" - it's a fancy hotel, and I had an account there - "and I'll see you in the morning at 8:30." I called up the hotel and said, "Reverend Reynolds is at the bus station; he's coming over for a room." They said, "Okay."

The next morning I got a call from the manager of the Hotel Charlotte, and he said, "Harry, what color is Reverend Reynolds?" And I said, "What color do you think he is?" He said, "The consensus of opinion is that he is a Negro." I said, "Well, he has already

---

*The Golden Vertical Plan was one of three satiric proposals suggested by Harry Golden as means of solving integration problems in the South. Golden noted that white Southerners historically rejected sitting next to blacks, but not standing alongside of them. Therefore, he called upon the public schools to immediately install stand-up desks which would keep everyone both vertical and satisfied. His second proposal was called the Golden Out-of-Order Plan. He had observed that whites would use drinking fountains maintained for blacks if the whites' facilities were not operating. An out-of-order sign, then, would be kept on white fountains until the need of separation was overcome. A third plan, the Golden Borrow-a-Child program, was suggested to eliminate segregated-seating at public events. Black maids escorting white children were admitted to white sections of theaters, Golden noted; therefore, centers could be established where white parents would deposit their ch children, saving sitter fees, and where blacks would borrow the children, allowing for integrated seating.

slept there; you can't make this retroactive, can you?
When he comes here at 8:30, I will call you back and I
will let you know what he is." He came at 8:30, and I
saw he was a Negro from Decatur, Georgia. He wanted to
stay another night, and it would be degrading to check
out of the hotel and look for a Negro rooming house.
So, I said, "Do you want to leave it to me?", and he
said, "Yes."

I called up the manager and said, "Mac, Reverend
Reynolds is here. He's not a Negro - he's a Hindu.
When a Hindu becomes a Christian, he takes his turban
off, and that's the reason this fellow doesn't have a
turban. You're lucky; you not only have a Hindu in the
hotel but a Methodist." So, when Reynolds got back
there he found a bowl of fruit in his room!

This gave me an idea. I wrote to Governor Hodges,*
who at that time was running up to Eisenhower every
week to try to cut down on the textile imports from
Japan which were threatening the textile industry in
North Carolina. He also was worried about Thurgood Marshall coming into the state and suing him for desegregation. I said, "You are worried about Thurgood Marshall and Japanese imports; I'll show you how you can
kill two birds with one stone. Give every Negro in

_____

*Luther Hodges, Governor of North Carolina from 1954
to 1960, later was Secretary of Commerce under presidents
Kennedy and Johnson. At the time of the 1954 Supreme
Court decision outlawing racial segregation in schools,
Hodges was considered a "moderate" in North Carolina and
an opponent of extremist white political elements which
called for the dissolving of the public education system. He was also among the first Southern governors to
seek large-scale financial investments in state industries by northern and even foreign entrepreneurs. Hodges' reward, on both counts, came in the form of the
position with the new national administration.

North Carolina a turban; it takes four and a half yards
of nylon to make one turban; the textile mills will run
night and day; you don't have to worry about Thurgood
Marshall because a Negro with a turban can go anywhere!"

It happened in 1943 I was to review a book in the
Christ Episcopal Church, the fanciest church in Charlotte, and before I reviewed the book I said, "Folks,
I've got a secret to tell you before I review this
book. If Jesus were to put Charlotte on his itinerary
during the second coming, I would be his contact man
here. In the first place, I'm a cousin; then he doesn't
talk this "you all" business and he would need an in-
terpreter; then he would need a social historian; he
would want to know what the hell the Episcopalians are,
and I could tell him."

It's good to be here. The most precious thing in
America is the college classroom, despite what you hear
around the country. This is the only precious thing
left in America, the college classroom. The press is
free, but the advertisers exert considerable influence
over it on the editorial policy and news columns. Television is free, but the sponsors write the programs.
The clergy is free, but the laymen have taken that over.
So, there is nothing left but the college classroom
where the professor locks the door and he and the kids
can go at it.

When the French Revolution exploded upon the world,
so great a man as Burke in England prophesied that it
would fail because of the insistence on equality. The
revolutionaries, warned Burke, went too far. Liberty
was firmly established in the Anglo-Saxon world; equality was a foreign and disturbing idea. Those Americans
who framed and fought for the new Constitution were
great men, some of the greatest men who ever lived.
Yet they did not mention equality in the Constitution.
They could not very well insist on equality, because
slavery was already an established institution in many

of the states. Tolerating slavery was one of the com-
promises these men had to make in order to insure creating a new nation. The Constitution when ratified in
1789 gave us liberty, the right to assemble, bear arms,
and speak out. It guaranteed a trial by jury, habeas
corpus, and it protected us against inhuman and excessive punishment. Equality for all waited until the
14th amendment, and it was ratified almost 100 years
later. Of equality, Benjamin Franklin said it was not
the work of one day.

It is obvious that men in the Western world have
resisted the notion of equality, the presumption that
all men are equal. They resist because their sense
tells them it is not true: all men are not created
equal. Some are richer than others, some are stronger,
some are smarter.

After the 14th Amendment was passed, the folks discovered that equality was a broad idea. Women were not
equal, and it took another 75 years before they were
certified as equal by a Constitutional Amendment. And
all the while that women struggled, men resisted. We
talk about the race riots in America, the burning of the
cities; this is nothing compared to woman's suffrage in
America. I saw white Protestant Anglo-Saxon women
dragged to the paddy wagon. They would chain themselves to a water hydrant in front of a Senator's home
who was against woman's suffrage, and the police were
called to detach them from the hydrants.

Alexander Hamilton was firmly convinced that only
the well-born and rich were fit to rule. His arguments
were more than sophisticated; they were persuasive. But,
Americans have chosen not to listen to these arguments.
We believe in log cabin presidents and slum-ascended
governors and consider ourselves better for them. Our
idea of equality however does not insist that all men
be reduced to a common denominator, for all men are equal
only in a slave state, save the masters. Our system of

private and individual initiative preserves the right
to accumulate wealth and property beyond the possessions
of all other men, the right of seniority, the rights of
preference and privilege.

But, during the past 15 years, we have witnessed
the struggle for other rights upon which we also insist
in theory: equality before the law; the right to participate in all public facilities; the right to compete
in the employment market on a fair basis; and the right
to live where you can pay the rent and conform to the
ordinary amenities of civilized people. Alas, with
these basic rights our practice has yet to catch up with
our theory.

Visit the prisons of America and you will come to
the conclusion that they are populated by the Negro and
the poor. They are thus populated not because of some
inherited racial trait among Negroes and poor whites
which lead them into a disproportionate amount of trouble
with the law, but because we deny them equality in the
courtroom. Many years ago Warden Lewis Lawes of Sing
Sing confessed that he had never electrocuted a rich man.
Indeed, only the poor pay for capital crimes with their
lives. Only now are people beginning to realize the
need to abolish capital punishment in order not to take
advantage solely of the poor and the friendless. Even
here, however, think of the resistance.

Equality has never been a popular cause. Today
there are law professors in our universities who are
unable to believe or bring themselves to face the con-
sequences of seeing that every man's vote is equal to
every other man's vote. One vote in upstate New York
is worth 30 votes downstate; one vote in eastern rural
North Carolina is worth 14 votes in the industrial Pied-
mont area. It took the Supreme Court almost 30 years
to see the inequity of this system. It has been the
inequitable distribution of legislative representatives
which has so inhibited the power of the individual states.

Now, what about the American Dream and the great
domestic problem today? Many well-meaning Americans
are asking a question today: "We gave them all they
asked for; what else do they want?" First, there is
an answer. The Negroes have asked for nothing that is
ours to give. They have asked for that which was
theirs the day they were born. But there is another
question which has not been fully articulated and which
is really at the bottom of the racial problem: "Should
the American Negro, for a limited period, receive more
than equal treatment in jobs, housing and the like to
make up for his long years of deprivation?" Let us
start with Abraham Lincoln: "If we knew where we are
and whither we are tending, we would better know what
to do and how to do it." Where are we, in relation to
this problem at this time? And, how about the uses of
the past?

I do not believe it would be fair to use the experience of other minority groups of our country as an
accurate analogy. Many people are doing this in an effort to wash their hands of the Negro movement, which
at this late date appears to be gaining momentum. I
was at Grossinger's, a very fancy resort in New York
state, a Jewish resort, and a lady said to me, "Why
do you always talk about civil rights, Mr. Golden; what
have the Negroes ever done for us and anyway, they're
anti-semitic." I said, "Lady, as soon as the Negroes
have a Grossinger's, I'll stop talking about Civil
Rights." I do not believe it would be fair to use the
experience of other minority groups in our country. I
was in the White House for three weeks writing my book,

*Mr. Kennedy and the Negroes,** and the President said,
"I'll see you every once in a while." I went in there
one day in March, 1963 and he said to me, "Two of my
close friends in the Senate were here yesterday, Smathers
from Florida and Russell of Georgia." They said to me,
"Mr. President, we saw your proposal for the 1963 Civil
Rights Laws. Why are the Negroes so special? Why do
they need this special legislation? The Irish came
here from the potato famine without a dime; the ads all
said no Irish need apply; they made it. There's one who
is President of the United States today. The Jews came
here from Eastern Europe without a dime; they went into
sweatshops and peddled from door to door and they made
it; they're in the middle class today. The Slavs, the
Hungarians and the Poles made it. They came from Eastern
Europe without a dime; they went into steel mills and
the coal pits; they made it. They're sending their sons
to the University of Pennsylvania today. Why are the
Negroes so special? Why can't they make it on their own?"
Kennedy smiled and he said, "You know what I told them?"
and he smiled, and I knew it was something good. He
said, "Gentlemen, you forgot one thing in your recital –
what an omission that is! Color. This man cannot move
from one place to another place and achieve any degree
of anonymity. He cannot change his name to hide his

---

*Mr. Golden's book, dedicated to the late President
as "our second 'Emancipator President'" explains in de-
tail the relation of both John and Robert Kennedy to
the growing black social revolution. It emphasizes the
political educative process which made the Kennedys
cognizant, as they had not been before, of the mon-
strousness of the social evils involved. Golden asserts
in the chapter entitled "Segregation and Treason" that
it was Robert Kennedy, often called the most political
of the two, who was to become the most personally involved as well. See MR. KENNEDY AND THE NEGROES, The
World Publishing Company, Cleveland and New York, chapter one.

origin. He must have legislation every step of the way,
and I mean to give it to him while I'm in the White
House."

The ghetto that I knew as a boy on the lower east
side of New York and the ghettoes that some of my
friends knew in Little Italy and in the Irish Hell's
Kitchen, as well as in Polishtown, were all filled with
hope despite the grinding poverty, the crowded tenements,
the bedbugs, the rats and the unsanitary conditions.
Our instinct told us that we could somehow get out. In
fact, we saw it happening every day. We knew that if
we studied hard, went to school and worked hard, we
could somehow jump the hurdles into the American mainstream. It is true that once you were there, you were
to encounter some pinpricks at the social level: you
couldn't join a club, maybe, or a fraternity or perhaps
get a reservation at certain resort hotels. But the
"restrictions" were nothing more than pinpricks. I
doubt seriously whether these annoyances prevented a
single one of us ghetto boys from burgeoning out a career based on merit, character, ambition, and talent.

But when we come to the American Negro minority,
we find the parallels of poverty, bedbugs, rats and
crowded tenements, but not the hope. That's where the
parallel ends. The Negro couldn't get out. Our society had established the political, educational, economic and social compulsions which kept him securely
locked in. And now they have all this civil rights
legislation. They can vote, go to the movies and to
the restrooms of the highway service stations. But they
remain securely locked away in their ghettoes. There
is some hope, of course, in the Negro ghetto of today,
but it is nothing like the hope we knew in the Irish,
Jewish, Italian, and Polish ghettoes of 1905.

My uncle struck it rich in America. He was a manufacturer of suspenders on Orchard Street on the north
east side. He was also a Notary Public. He had a big

star outside his little factory. In those days you had
to get working papers. You had to be 14 years old. You
went to a Notary Public, and he signed this certificate
that you were 14 years old. But if you were 11 years
old and wanted to go to work, you went to my uncle anyway. He would give you a certificate for a quarter.
He was a pioneer. He moved up to Riverside Drive, the
most beautiful street in New York, one of the most
beautiful streets in the world. In 1910, he moved up
there. It wasn't his fault that the Gentiles moved out;
he just wanted to look at the Hudson River, that's all.
The Gentiles moved out and they went over to the east
side and cleaned that up, cleaned up the old city dump
and built their beautiful apartment houses and moved
in. And a year later the Jews followed them to the east
side. The Gentiles figured, "We'll get the Jews now;
we'll move out to Long Island. There are no delica-
tessen stores out there." So they moved out to Long
Island; they came along and built a subway to Long Island and the Jews followed them to Long Island!

In Miami there was hand-to-hand fighting, block by
block. The Gentiles held out on Fifteenth Street for
10 years. The Gentiles made the same mistake that the
British made in Singapore. They figured, "Where is the
enemy coming from? From the sea." So, they pointed
their guns at the sea. But the enemy came from behind
them, from the jungle. The Gentiles figured, "We're
trying to run away from the Jews. So where are the
Jews coming from? New York." They faced towards New
York, but the Jews came from the west. They outflanked
the Gentiles!

Here's another example: the owner of the leading
department store in my city made a frantic call on me one
evening. The Negro students were picketing his establishment. He thought I could do something to help remove
the pickets. "I do not mind desegregating my basement
snack bar but I will never desegregate my Tulip Room -
tell them that," said the department store head. His

Tulip Room is on a beautiful roof garden overlooking the city, where the leading citizens come for lunch. I said to him, "If I were you, I would desegregate the Tulip Room tomorrow. How many Negroes are there in Charlotte who can pay you $4.00 for lunch?" His jaw dropped. He had never heard that argument. The next morning he de-segregated his Tulip Room, and such was his prestige that all the other establishments gave up the resistance, and the amazed pickets went back to their classes. I called him six or seven months later, asked him if he had served a Negro customer in the Tulip Room yet. He laughed and said that a local banker had had two Negro guests up from Atlanta a few months before.

We Jews could go from the crowded filthy tenements of the lower east side to the Tulip Rooms of Broadway and to Riverside Drive and to other nice sections of the city to live because we had reached the economic level at which we could pay the rent: we could pay the check at the Tulip Room and pay the rent in Washington Heights. The Irish moved from Hell's Kitchen up to Amsterdam Avenue when the sons of the Irish immigrants began to fill the jobs of policemen, bailiffs, court clerks and conductors on the subways and the Fifth Av-enue bus. The Italians moved from Little Italy to Staten Island when they had achieved some degree of economic success.

I have a strong suspicion that the Gentiles up on Riverside Drive and on Washington Heights were as deeply chagrined to see us come into the neighborhood as are the whites of Chicago, Cleveland and New York when they see the Negroes parading near their residences. But we could pay the rent and, because we could pay the rent, the only thing the Gentiles could do was move out. We did not like to see this, but there was nothing we could do about it except wave them goodbye. After all, we were not chasing them. We were not particularly anxious to live next door to them; all we were anxious to do was get out of the ghetto. A better place for the children,

our parents said. But the key to this situation was that
we could pay the rent. Indeed, what good is open housing if you can't pay the rent?

None of the economic, political and educational compulsions which have kept the Negro locked in affected us.
At age 12, we went out and got our first job as an er-
rand boy. I never saw a Negro fellow-employee in all
those years on eight or 10 different jobs. And let us
remember that we all have kept the Negroes locked in
during the 75 years of the greatest wealth-producing
period in the history of the world, a period such as we
will never see again.

We can reasonably say that we lost a war and that
an indemnity should be paid. We lost the war to the
Negro, kept him invisible; but he's no longer invisible,
he's burning our cities. This is an indemnity not to
a victorious foreign power, but an indemnity paid to
ourselves. This is money we would get back ten-fold
within two generations. Out of 23 million Negroes in
America at least 15 million are entitled to some "back
pay." The payment of an indemnity, therefore, would
build for us a new gulf stream of vitality. Suppose we
get only one Charles Steinmetz* out of it, or only one
George Washington Carver out of the children of those
15 million? Only one Charles Steinmetz or only one
George Washington Carver would be enough to cancel the
entire loan. We are dealing with human resources. We
must bear that in mind.

_____

*1865-1923; investigator of magnetism and of light-
ening phenomena, who came to the United States in 1899
after experiencing difficulties with foreign authorities
because of his political socialism. Steinmetz eventually
taught electrical engineering at Union College in Schnec-
tady and wrote several volumes in that field including
ENGINEERING MATHEMATICS and FOUR LECTURES ON RELATIVITY
AND SPACE.

In 1948, we instituted a Marshall Plan to aid the
war-torn countries of Europe. This was a step unparal-
leled in human history. In recent years, we have
stretched out our arms (in employment, education and
welfare) to Hungarian and Cuban refugees. Our G.I.
Bill of Rights after World War II was, in a sense, a
recognition of a special need of a special segment of
our population. That is precedent enough if we must
have a precedent.

Let us remember, too, that life is a struggle
under most normal conditions. But, in addition to the
ordinary forces affecting one's way of life, the Negro's
struggle into the American mainstream has been thwarted
by discrimination, segregation and denial based on the
color of his skin. We can almost prove this methodi-
cally. (So few reporters and sociologists have explored
this area of Negro life.) Did you know, for example,
that in 1964 at the height of the greatest prosperity
the world has ever known anywhere, the third biggest
killer in 14 of our states was pregnancy - Negro pregnancy? Five Negro women died in childbirth to one white
woman; Negro infant mortality was five and a half times
greater than white infant mortality. Tuberculosis,
fourteenth as a cause of death among whites, was second
as the cause of death among Negroes. Most of our immigrant groups could say to their children, "America
offers you political, educational and economic freedom -
go to it." The Negro parents could never tell their
children, "Go to it."

Thus, I believe we must have a subsidy, a loan.
The direction of the racial problem of America today
must combine the elements of the crash program, a domestic Marshall Plan, perhaps not less than one hundred
billion dollars over the next ten years. It would establish a planned effort to place qualified Negroes in
all categories of employment, at all levels of responsibility. Labor unions would have to make a conscientious
effort to include Negroes in their membership and training programs. The Building Trades, for example, where

where few Negroes have been employed in the past, would
be called upon to offer a conscious preferment to help
the Negro catch up. And this "conscious preferment"
must obtain in all areas of employment of our country
where Negroes have not been employed in the past.

We must have the money to provide necessary inten-
sified remedial instruction in the lower grades for culturally deprived and retarded pupils. Schools and colleges must have the resources to find new ways to seek
out Negro youths with undeveloped talents. Similarly,
adult education among Negroes on a broad scale must be
geared to the needs of citizens lacking the basic lit-
erary and technical skills. Education is a key to the
entire problem. There must be a broad-based program of
education from kindergarten to the grad school.

None of this will carry with it the idea of exempt-
ing the Negro from the independence and the initiative
demanded by our free, competitive society. But, such
a program would make practical economic sense as a
measure to reduce unemployment and welfare costs and to
increase productivity and national income while it
helped the Negro catch up in the benefits of our rich
society. President Johnson's economic advisors had estimated that our gross national product could be raised
nearly three per cent were the Negro workers' earnings
commensurate with the national average. Furthermore,
such a domestic Marshall Plan as I am proposing would
have profound moral and religious justification.

Education is a key to the entire problem. Education.
The Jews were in the ghettoes for 1500 years. They survived. When the ghetto walls came down by Napoleon in
1805, the Jews were bewildered. They still lived in a
hostile world. One-third of the Jews in Berlin became
Christians, not out of conviction but out of frustration
and fear. Then, suddenly in the middle of the 19th Century, they got onto a trick. They learned a gimmick.
They made a wild dash to the universities of Europe, and

they are still dashing to the universities of America.
When the Jewish boys couldn't get in the University of
Paris, they studied their books, nearby under candle-
light, figuring that being next to the edifice would•
psychologically help them.

Let us remember, too, that the Negro movement in
America has been unique in the history of social revolutions, probably the only "revolution" in history which
did not demand alteration of a single existing institution. The American Negro is in revolt, not to change
the fabric of our society or to seek a special place in
it, but in the hope of entering the mainstream and
achieving a full participation in all the wonders of
American life. All we need now is the wisdom to follow
through. We know from our past history our sense of
decency and fair play. The poet Arthur Hugh Clough*
wrote over 100 years ago:

> And not by eastern windows only,
> When daylight comes,
>   comes in the light.
> In front the sun climbs slow, how slowly,
> But westward, look, the land is bright.

But the resistance continues, not only in the deep
South, but in our large cities. And it continues only
because of the need for a caste system. We have won-
derful projects privately financed for research: polio,
heart, cancer, tuberculosis, muscular dystrophy, all
worthwhile projects that perform great good to the
people. But the third biggest killer in fourteen states

---

*English poet, 1819-1861, best known as the author
of "Say not, the struggle nought availeth" and for the
melancholy expression of religious conflicts in works
such as "Mari Magnon" (1849) and "Dipsychus" (1849), a
series of dialogues between Faust and the Satan image.

is Negro pregnancy. There are no drives for that. In
fact, no research is even necessary. We have the facilities and the know-how to remedy the situation, a
situation due to segregation and discrimination. To the
eternal credit of the south, it must be said that not a
single reputable doctor or scientist or pathologist in
America has come out of the university and tried to jus-
tify segregation on biological grounds. Only the politicians have spoken. They have a vested interest in
segregation.

What is actually involved is the recognition of
humanity. Because above all else is human dignity. A
human being can go without food longer than he can go
without human dignity. Here is a true story: there was
an intelligence test for Negro children as part of an
anti-poverty project. One of the pictures on the paper
was of a window with a crack in it. "What's wrong with
this picture?" was the question. And none of the Negro
children gave the answer. A crack in a window was not
a wrong to them. They had cardboard for windows, or
rags, or they had no windows at all. Thus, we have
succeeded in this past century to strip these people
of human dignity.

Mr. Larkin, a welfare director in North Carolina
who is a Negro, took me out one day last August to investigate some illegitimacy, and he said to me, "Let's
stop at my uncle's farm. The old gent came up to the
gate, and we chatted. I was dying to get in the house
to get into the shade and get a drink of water, but he
didn't invite us in. Finally, we went away and Larkin
said to me," "I suppose you're wondering why he didn't
invite us in the house." I said, "Yes, I am wondering
about it." He said the old man wanted to get a baby
grand piano for his daughters, and he'd be damned if
he'd let a white man see that he's got a baby grand
piano. This is how we've de-humanized the people, de-
humanized them completely.

These are the common enemies which underlie all
forms of tyranny: racism, authoritarianism, McCarthyism.
They are no less enemies when being sold or offered as
truth or salvation by blacks, yellows or whites. If
Negroes and whites who understand this can make it
clear, we can help save America. We will use the power
of disciplined intelligence combined with respect for
moral values and humanity to save Negroes from destruction and from the possibilities of white and black dilemmas and thereby contribute to the survival of America. For America - listen to this; I believe this
from the bottom of my heart - America cannot survive
if the Negroes do not. Remember this! America cannot
survive if the Negroes do not. And, Negroes and no
other group of human beings are likely to survive if
America does not.

White racism is the great disease of America today.
We must somehow break the cycle of white   . Primitive legislation will never do it. More police, more
vigilantes; these have never worked in the history of
man. There has to be progressive legislation, a Marshall Plan. The conservatives, the fellows on the far
right, believe that history goes up in a straight line
without any turning or deviation. This straight line
of history theory they call "The American Way of Life."
Well, much could be said about that American way of life.
It took its most drastic turn when we discovered the
Mesabi range and Iron Mountain* which became the steel

---

*Excavations at Iron Mountain were begun in 1845.
Located on the southern spur of the St. Francois Moun-
tins in Missouri, this deposit of hematite iron ore
was recognized as the purest in the United States. The
Mesabi Range was opened in 1890, and its location in
northeastern Minnesota proved to be one of the largest,
most accessible iron deposits in the world. During the
twentieth century, nearly half of the iron ore mined a
and used in the country has come from the Mesabi area.

industry, and we changed from a crude agricultural way
of life to an industrial and urban way of life with a
million problems every 24 hours.

Once you could print your own money. If you owned
a bank, you could do your own printing. In 1860, there
were so many different kinds of money that you had to
get it validated from state to state. That "American
way of life" changed with the introduction of the
National Bank Act.

Once you could run a railroad anywhere you wanted
to. You could charge what you wanted to charge. You
could take the goods from one shipper and tell another
shipper, "nothing doing." That American way of life
gave way to a new American way of life when the government stepped in and acted as a referee over the railroad business.

Once you could open a store and sell what merchandise you pleased, charge what you wanted to charge, and
tell your employees when to come and when to quit, pay
them what you wanted to pay them. That American way
of life changed. You have to get a license to operate
a store. Your wiring has to be approved before you can
open up. The government counts your employees and tells
you that there is a minimum wage for them. You must
pay them overtime after a certain number of hours, and
the government tells you that you must not only pay your
own taxes but you must collect taxes for the government.
The government tells you that you must serve everyone
that comes in regardless of his color. That's the new
American way of life.

When I was a kid in school and the teacher mentioned France, we thought of Joan of Arc or LaFayette.
When she mentioned England, we thought of King Henry
the Eighth with all his wives. Today it's a different
American way of life. A way of life that requires total awareness and total commitment. This is what the

kids in the universities are howling about, because
they know; they are highly aware today. They know all
about Asia and Africa and the Middle East. You can't
kid them anymore. You can't kid them with Joan of Arc.
They know all about her. They know that there are men
with strange names and countries with names they can't
even pronounce that could say or do something tomorrow
which could very well determine the kind of life they
will lead. This requires total awareness and total
commitment. That's a new American way of life.

Senator Strom Thurmond, if you would pardon the
expression, says that if you contribute federal monies
to a public education you will deprive the people of
free enterprise and private initiative. George Wallace
echoes the same thing. George Wallace says that the
business of education is nobody's business but
Alabama's. But, there is a new way of American life
today. Today, when you spit on a Negro kid in Alabama,
it's pictured on the front page of every newspaper in
the world, not only the Communist press but the press
of our friends in the neutral nations. Wallace is
wrong when he says it's the business of Alabama; it's
our business in Georgia and in New York and everywhere
else.

The conservatives say that federal aid to education will destroy private initiative. They say it
on the same day when the federal government pours
billions of dollars into Alabama and South Carolina.
Indeed, the entire South has been one federal preserve
in the last 40 years, like National Yellowstone Park
except with people. It gets a check every day from
the federal government: the soil bank, farm subsidies,
a check for social security, veterans' pay, welfare;
checks for roads, airports, army camps, checks for
laboratories, industries. It gets the checks from the
federal government, and it cashes the checks, and it
says the government is getting too big!

We must break the cycle of white racism in
America because this can divide a country down the
middle, and we will have guerilla warfare before it's
over. White racism is terrible. It bespeaks man's
other nature; the fear of the stranger, the fear of
rocking the boat. The churches backed away from the
moral issue in 1954. Martin Luther King came along
and saved the Protestant churches of America in the
South when he said, "If blood is to flow in the
streets of Birmingham, make sure it's our blood and
not the blood of our white brothers." Who else has
said anything like that? Somehow we must find a
balance between the wonders of science and the greater
wonders of human kindness. We must find a balance between the miracles of technology and the miracle of
human kindness. This is the greatest virtue of all,
human kindness.

John Birchers said impeach Earl Warren. Well,
he's left now. There was a big poster in Atlanta -
IMPEACH EARL WARREN - The John Birch Society. They
never mentioned the real villain, Justice Fred Vinson.
It was Fred Vinson who set the pattern for the Negro
revolution of the 1950's. While Earl Warren was still
Governor of California, Fred Vinson set the pattern.
The Negroes, mind you, just never challenged the separate idea; they never said, "We want to be with the
whites." They only challenged equal.* "It's not
equal", they said.

---

*The inequalities of southern black and white
educational facilities increased rather than diminished
during the early part of the twentieth century. In
1900, southern states were spending three dollars on
education for each white to two dollars for each black
child; by 1930, a white student received seven dollars
worth of education to two dollars worth for a black.

In Clarendon County, South Carolina where the kids go
to school, they had to pick up kindling for the pot-
bellied stove, the roof leaked, and there was no
library, while the white school had a library with
everything else. "It's not equal," they said. Fred
Vinson claimed, "Separate is the evil thing." He
said, "Facilities have nothing to do with it. You can
give the Negroes gold doorknobs and a private tutor
for every student, but if you keep them separate this
is unequal education. Because education involves the
prestige of the alumni, the size of the library, but
most of important of all, the ability to communicate
with other students."

We are what we are because of the classmates we
met in school. We are not conscious of this, of
course, but every adult in this room has gotten his
patterns of speech, his patterns of behavior, from
his classmates. When you separate the people, you are
denying them equal education. Justice Vinson said in
the case against the Texas Law School for Negroes,

The challenge to unequal facilities took strength
after 1935 when a Maryland Court of Appeals ruled
that out-of-state tuition grants to blacks were a
violation of equal protection of the laws, and in
1938 when the Supreme Court supported this decision
by claiming that equal facilities had to be provided
within a state. It was following these cases that the
older Plessy v. Ferguson doctrine of "separate but
equal" was more tangibly supported by southern states
which began wide-scale construction of black colleges
and graduate schools. But, as Mr. Golden suggests,
it was not until Justice Vinson's rulings that the
14th Amendment was used to successfully reverse the
notion that separate could be equal.

"You are keeping Negro law students away from their
colleagues whom they will meet in the courtroom some
day; their colleagues who will be the judges and the
prosecutors, the opposing lawyers in a suit, and this
is unequal education."*

The Jews were in the ghettoes for 1500 years and
they survived, and they produced some biblical
scholars, the Talmudists. But quite frankly, each day
was like the other day until the walls of the ghetto
came down. Then, they were able to exchange ideas
with the western man. It was then that you got your
Brandeis,Disraeli, Jonas Salk: the interchange of
ideas with the rest of civilization is what did it
for them.

We must find this balance between the miracle of
technology and the miracle of human kindness in a new
American Way of Life.

---

*The case, Sweatt v. Painter, was ruled on in 1950
and claimed, specifically, that a segregated law school
for Negroes in Texas could not be considered equal to
the University of Texas Law School since segregation
per se was a major factor in making for inequality.
This particular decision encouraged the N.A.A.C.P. to
file an expanded series of cases to eradicate separate
public school systems generally which led, in turn, to
the May 17, 1954 unanimous Supreme Court decision in
Brown v. the Board of Education of Topeka.

DIALOGUE WITH HARRY GOLDEN

QUESTIONER: I notice that you put education first.
Why?

MR. GOLDEN: Education is the key to life in the civilized world. Education is the big problem among the
Negroes of America. Once you get an education, you've
got it made. You can enter into the mainstream of civilization. Education is the most significant single aspect of a new American way of life.

QUESTIONER: You said that the only way America could
survive is to let the Negro survive and vice versa,
and you related several experiences of the Jews being
oppressed. But, they were constantly rising up. Does
the black experience offer a basis for blacks rising
up in America?

MR. GOLDEN: The black experience is unique. The
Jews came from East Europe, from an urban society.
The early church fathers put them in the ghettoes,
thinking it as punishment; they didn't realize they
were giving the Jews a 1500-year head start in how to
live in the urban society of the 20th century. The
Negro came from a plantation, an agricultural society;
entirely different. Thus, he has to catch up in
entirely different ways.

QUESTIONER: How can we break this cycle of white
racism to which you referred, in the face of increasing
polarization between the races?

MR. GOLDEN: This is a sad thing, because the extremists
among the Negroes are doing it wrong. They are arguing
with the professors in the universities; they want
soul poetry. What the hell would they do with soul
poetry when they need composition or arithmetic?
Soul poetry they want!

QUESTIONER: Well who, then, can break this cycle?

MR. GOLDEN: It's up to the whites to break the cycle
of the white racism. This is a white problem which
whites must solve.

QUESTIONER: Would you please comment on the recent
manifestation of anti-semitism among blacks?

MR. GOLDEN: This has been exaggerated, completely
exaggerated. The Negroes of America are not anti-
semites. I have vast communication with them.
Neither are their leaders: Bayard Rustin isn't; A.
Phillip Randolph isn't; Dr. King wasn't; Roy Wilkins
isn't; Whitney Young isn't: none of these people are
anti-semites. You have a small group of extremists
who use this thing, but a Negro anti-semite is about
as convincing as a Jewish white supremist!

Also, I feel that the extremists on the campus
are wrong demanding private, separate dormitories and
separate classrooms and separate teachers. They are
completely wrong, because this is a pluralistic society. We are not Jewish Americans; we are Americans
who happen to be Jewish. We are Americans who happen
to be Irish; we are Americans who happen to be Negroes.
It's the only chance we've got in a pluralistic society, being totally integrated.

QUESTIONER: In order for America to be a pluralistic
society, it seems the society would have to continue
to develop many local spectrums. If so, do you still
describe this in terms of "The American Way of Life?"

MR. GOLDEN: The American way of life took many drastic
turns, as I have pointed out, and has experienced constant change. The American way of life in the fore-
seeable future will be a life of whites and Negroes
together. This will be the new American way of life.
We are coming to that now. The Supreme Court has

given us the laws, and morals follow the law; don't
ever mistake that. Those who say the laws can't do
it deny the entire Anglo-Saxon ethos. If you ask a
Welsh miner or sheep herder in the Hebrides, "Do you
want the Catholics to .." "What the hell do I care
about 'the Catholics', 'the Pope will come over here',
and all this business?" We have seen a miracle, the
changing of the whole social order of the South within
15 years.

I remember when the Governor of South Carolina
said, "Blood will flow in the streets in South
Carolina if we desegregate." No blood flowed. They
graduate in schools. It's a miracle! This is America!
This is what makes America so great: a rigid social
order that existed for a hundred years has changed.

When I first came to Charlotte, North Carolina,
I saw Negroes step off the sidewalks and let a white
man pass. But they are not stepping off the sidewalks
today; they are tripping along the sidewalks with
their daughters, taking them to dancing schools.
Negroes are all over the place: they are in the city
council; they are in the Community Chest; they are in
every city bureau in every city agency. And they will
go further yet; they will go much further. You have
over 80 Negro office holders in the South today.
This was unheard of 15 or 18 years ago. A Negro
couldn't vote in Alabama or Mississippi, or in
Georgia. This is the way history will treat this, as
the changing of a social order in 15 years. This is
the great miracle of America. You mustn't downgrade
it. You must be enthused about it!

QUESTIONER: Jews represent to black people an immediate oppressor. In New York City, the Jew has taken
over the total educational system. You speak of getting education, but we have to get it through the
Jews, and this is what I consider a form of colonialism.

In the communities where we live, the immediate
oppressor is the Jew who owns the store. He is the
person who has jacked up his prices five cents a box
higher than the super market. So the Jew, basically
in the black community, is the oppressor. You said
that black people aren't anti-semitic, and you mentioned A. Phillip Randolph and Bayard Rustin. These
people are no longer considered spokesmen for the
black community. They are considered Uncle Toms or
first-class fools.

So, you kind of left me when you said that
black people are not anti-semitic, because we are.
The only reason that you might not know this is because we don't tell you the truth! Would you comment
on this?

MR. GOLDEN: Black people of America are not anti-
semitic. They know that the Jews were first in line
to help them. They know that the Jews contributed
first to the Civil Rights Movement, that Jewish boys
were killed in Mississippi working for the Negroes.
They know this. The Negroes aren't fools. I won't
deny that there are Jewish slumlords in Harlem. I
won't deny that there are Jewish storekeepers who
overcharge. But Negro reaction is aggression against
the whites not against the Jews. The Jews happen to
be handy to represent the whites.

The greatest slumlords in the world are from
the South. In every Southern town there are fellows
who have so-called "nigger houses." These slumlords
are the second richest men in town, next to those in
the Coca-Cola industry. They are white, Protestant,
Anglo-Saxon owners of these houses in the South, and
they are financed by white, Protestant banks. They
are the primary oppressor.

REVOLUTION AND THE LIBERAL EXPLOITER

William Osborne

The mere mention of rape makes Richard Nixon's middle America think black. Rape is not just an anti-social act in which one seizes by force something not freely given, rape is lower class, ethnic, distinct-ively black. Rape may occur within ghettos, but that context for the event is unimportant. What must always be remembered is that rapacious blacks have an ultimate goal of victimizing the innocent, powerless white. This middle American rationale depends upon elaborate sexual mythologies first developed out of the slavemaster's paranoia, but it is significant in present history because of the resulting actions taken by white folk. Good Baptist ladies in Mississippi who sing on Sundays about Jesus loving all the little children, place shotguns by their bedsides at night to ward off lecherous black intruders; junior executives in Michigan who are ambiguous about American wars in southeast Asia form para-military societies at home in order to prevent suspected black advances. For middle America, if there is a rape of the powerless, the per-petrator is clearly black.

The mention of rape makes the black intellectual think white. He finds his community totally altered by the anti-social act. His people are colors which they never carried with them from home shores; his group experiences a caste status out of which none of the brothers can climb; and he describes this dilemma with his own creative terms such as "motherfucker,"

which literally tells the story. For the black, who
must find meaning in Turner, Dubois, Malcolm and Fanon,
rape takes on dimensions far beyond interpersonal sexual exploitation: it defines the relation of a domi-
nating community to the dominated, and it character-
izes the success at exploitation the white society has
enjoyed for 350 years. For the black, there is a rape
of the powerless, and the perpetrator is clearly the
total white community.

The mention of a rape of the powerless makes the
white liberal turn paler but not more liberal. His
sophistication does not allow him to categorize blacks
so easily as the middle Americans do but his whiteness
prevents him from accepting a harsh and generalized
indictment of his own group by blacks. The liberal
simply does not care to think in terms of rape or
powerlessness, for these are the emotive words used by
the passionate, and they suggest the very kind of im-
passe liberals seek to avoid. The liberal cannot cope
with the concepts behind such dramatic rhetoric since
his whole life style is based on the possibility of the
absence of radical confrontation. He bemoans polarization and tries to forget that it has been happening
since before the founding of the nation; he promotes
the myth of togetherness which neither middle America
nor the ethnic minorities have ever experienced; he
luxuriates in a progressive interpretation of history
for which there is no evidence. When American life is
interpreted in terms of rape and powerlessness, the
liberal posture has to be one of withdrawal from the
dialogue, for his bases of conversation and action do
not include such severity.

This typical withdrawal from confrontation makes
it clear in the 1970's that liberalism is a luxury
which only the affluent whites of this nation can
afford. It is political indulgence of the comfortable,
those who have the resources which allow for reflection, protracted debate and ultimate compromise.

Liberalism is that social ethic which assumes that
passion is dangerous, that reason is an adequate vehicle for decision-making, that social structures are
being made more responsive to peoples' needs, that
rape need not happen, and that powerlessness is not
the problem. The liberal's *modus operandi* is the high
hope, and this is clearly distinguishable from that of
the middle American who is largely fearful, or the
black who is frustrated, or the times generally which
are composed of unrelenting conflicts of power between
groups. The white liberal's politics of cheerfulness
are out of step with the times and cannot be related
to contemporary events. Further, the irrelevance of
liberal politics must not be interpreted as being
merely unfortunate but, rather, as part of the total
white community's exploitation of the oppressed and a
frustration of rapid social change.

The white liberal, of course, is astonished when
identified as an exploiter, a participant in the rape of
groups. He interprets his historical past and the future in terms of necessary and universal human ideals
whose relevance is guaranteed. He asks how charges of
exploitation can be credible when liberal tradition
depends upon Jefferson affirmations of equality,
Jackson's populist orientation, Lincoln's interest in
emancipation or Wilson's vision of one world. Or, how
could this nation humanely survive in the 1970's and
beyond apart from these principles? But the very asking of the question - particularly when it is the oppressed who are asked - becomes an exploitive act. For
what are historic principles to one who only knows
economic deprivation, one who is politically powerless
one who has experienced cultural rape when the arti-
facts of his society were seized by force and obliterated? What is this liberal recourse to principle
when existence has become the survival of the fittest
and a working out of one's own salvation without success? How can comfortable abstractions be verbalized

to communities whose life is so agonizing that there
is no commonality with the ideal? How can liberal
tradition be meaningly referred to when Jefferson did
not attempt to establish equality, when Jackson's pop-
ulism has been taken over by southern demagogues, when
Lincoln only produced a paper emancipation, and when
the militarists have carved out many worlds, not one,
in Wilson's time and our own? The liberal recourse to
the ideal is a cruel refuge into which most Americans
are not qualified to enter, a refuge always identified
in suitably non-concrete terms and presided over by
the defining liberal himself. To rephrase the ancient
prophet, the liberal's ideal is the stone he offers to
the exploited when they cry out for the meat of a new
existence. In this instance Marx was correct: the
bourgeoisie provide abstractions which in fact opiate
the masses.

The general recognition of the liberal ubterfuge
is a recent phenomenon on the American political scene.
There have always been occasional radical actors or
intellectuals who expressed suspicion of liberal ideals
such as leaders of slave revolts, some left-wing abolitionists, later black militants during the Garvey era,
and the American Communists of the 1930's some of whom
indulged in their own irrelevant dreams. But mass rejection of the white liberal awaited a recent historical event, the murder of Martin Luther King, Jr. For
many blacks and few whites, this occurrence has acted
as the catalyst in the refashioning of relations.

I recall two incidents which revealed for me the
new or renewed rejection of the white liberal. In
1963, a black student whom I had never seen before
banged on my office door shouting, "Professor Osborne!
Cut your radio on: the President has been shot." The
student and I sat together for three quarters of an
hour until the media finally told the truth. The
President had not just been shot; John Kennedy was

dead and had been for some time. Neither of us said a
word. It wasn't necessary. Rather, that curious feeling of empathy which needs no language permeated the
room until both the student and I walked out of the
door without meeting again. Five years later, however,
there was no knock on my door, no sitting down with a
student, no curious feeling of empathy. The murder of
Martin Luther King did not allow for implications of
togetherness, common suffering, or the sense of misery
needing my company. The dying of the black prophet,
instead, resignalled the clear delineation of black
and white and the impossibility of the fragile, deceptive idealisms which had characterized the liberal
past. On the black campus at which I taught, King's
murder did not issue into the singing of "We Shall
Overcome" since there was a consensus of feeling that
the "We" in the freedom hymn was not really the black
man at all but the white liberal who through his use of
blacks and others had already overcome! Thus, the
death of King has become one of those clarifying events
in history where people begin to redefine en masse who
they are in relation to others. And this event in particular has overcome the image of the white liberal as
a kind of anti-hero, a bungler whose political inept-
ness is obvious but who, nevertheless, is the servant
of good causes; a man who might succeed without really
trying. Instead, the liberal's response to King's
death - words of self-reproach and no actions of consequence - have exposed him as the comfortable one who
can live with or without the prophets and still cling
to his abstractions which he doesn't need to have
socially realized.

American liberal culture has never adequately
groped with social catastrophe, because it hasn't had
to. This culture is the outlook of a privileged class
group within the social structure, the bourgeoisie.
Since the bourgeoisie or upper middle segments in
America have been on the financial and political as-
cendency, it has been to their advantage to avoid power

confrontations with other groups and to claim that such
struggles were unnecessary in order to secure justice
and equality. Any radical re-ordering of society, such
as that attempted presently in America by black and
white revolutionaries, means the end of liberal cultural dominance, the suppression of liberal financial
greed, and the exposure of deceptive liberal senti-
mentalities. The American political liberal is a product of the same forces which the contributors to this
volume challenge as being socially detrimental. The
liberal would not exist without the structures of the
self-serving corporations Ralph Nader describes; or
the white Protestant banking interests mentioned by
Harry Golden; or the university superstructures
against which Mark Rudd has struggled; or the racist
urban majorities alluded to by Julian Bond and Ivan
Allen; or the retrogressing national administrations
described by Mrs. Chisholm. The liberal is part and
parcel of that system which he ostensibly fights but
whose fruits he enjoys; the eradication of the system
would mean the removal of the liberal's prestigous position, the end of the comfort which allows for his
political dilettantism.

That the liberal is a party to the rape of the
powerless does not necessarily signify his consciousness of this participation. Instead, the underlying
assumptions to liberal thought and action are so erroneous from the outset that the question of consciousness of an exploitive role is largely beside the point.
It really doesn't matter whether or not the liberal's
self-conception correlates with the historical reality
of his actions, or whether he does or does not admit to
his involvements which negate the interests of the
larger community. Societal change cannot depend upon
the conversion of the oppressor; a social action must
not be justified on the basis of helping the oppressor
to admit his inhuman conduct. The King movements had
to learn the hard way that leading lambs to the slaugh-
ter does not necessarily create the expected or hoped
for feelings of guilt in the slaughterer. Therefore,
the liberal ideology must be exposed without liberal
help. It must be viewed as a self-serving weapon used

against other classes and groups in order to continue
liberal dominance, a weapon whose assumptions are deceptive for and frustrating to those groups whose basic
need is social power.

Most importantly, the white liberal misleadingly
assumes the goodness of human nature and, in particular,
his own identification with this goodness. It is this
estimate of the very being of man which leads the liberal to an overly optimistic expectation of human actions. The liberal rejects the position that man is in
any fundamental sense a problem to himself or his own
worst enemy. Specifically, the liberal has been offended by religious anthropologies which claimed that
man's make-up includes a reticence to do good and, perhaps, a tendency toward the negative. In place of such
pessimism, the liberal has constructed an interpretation of man which has antecedents in Greek philosophy
and, more recently, continues the Renaissance affirmation that there is a plasticity about human beings which
allows their being shaped and modified into more perfect
social actors. In the realities of present historical
events, however, this estimate of human nature tends to
be a sentimental obscuring of the social truth and, beyond that, the attempt to obscure must be recognized as
the weapon of a knowing or unknowing exploiter. Not on
only do the conditions of men in general not allow for
such optimism, but the optimist reveals that he does not
consider these conditions with seriousness. This liberal assumption of the goodness of man, if accepted by
the oppressed, becomes a barrier to their understanding
of the radically negative powers they must confront in
order to overcome oppression.

I am not suggesting a return to Hobbes or
Machiavelli as an alternative to liberal optimism,
rather it would be far more accurate to view the human
expression dialectically, that is as an interplay between
contradictory emphases of good and evil, meaning and
non-meaning. While the understanding of such paradox

may take a bit of sophistication, the liberal claims
to be the sophisticated analyst in contemporary society! It is quite possible to recognize the contradictory qualities of man in present American history.
A Richard Nixon who woos the southern racists also
suggests a minimum family income plan; Lyndon Johnson
who radically escalated the war in Vietnam also coerced
a recalcitrant Congress to pass protective domestic social legislation; Robert Kennedy who walked among the
grape pickers was careful to maintain his alliances
with big city bosses; Elijah Muhammad delineates an
ontology of all whites as devils but also provides a
community of national expectation for his black followers; the liberal himself whose verbiage about justice makes for theoretical pleasantness issues that
verbiage out of the continuation of an unjust system
on which he depends. It is too easy and too diverting
to define man, as the liberal does, as good. Man, on
the basis of his acts, must be viewed as a complexity
of good and evil from which something is required while
too much is not expected. Man in American society is
both destroyer and contributor, to be viewed with suspicion and hope simultaneously.

        The white liberal further assumes that human good-
ness finds its most adequate expression in reason and
that, if men would be rational about their differences,
solutions to social problems would be found. Lyndon
Johnson's plea, "Come let us reason together" epit-
omizes the liberal overevaluation of the integrity of
reason although Johnson in fact wielded the necessary
power to make that reasoning process work to his advantage. The liberal, however, errs in a naive deifi-
cation of reason which is but one exercise of man who,
as I am affirming, is qualitatively good and evil in
the use of all faculties. Therefore, reason is not
always dependable; it is dependent upon and in the
service of the more complex motivations of man. To
quote Luther, "Reason is a whore!"

The liberal's reliance upon reason as the vehicle
to community progress is evidence of his ignorance of
the cultures of the oppressed about him. The re-emerg-
ing concept of "soul" in American black society, for
example, finds African roots which are unaffected by
western interpretations of reason. Rather, "soul" refers to an established commonality of feeling and purpose of a people creating its community apart from mere
rational explanations. There is serious identity
built about the feeling-knowledge of "soul" although
the experience may be considered irrational or non-
rational by western, liberal criteria. The same could
be said of the group identity of the American Indians,
Chinese Americans and, to some extent, the chicanos.
The white liberal's dependence upon reason becomes at
best an oversimplification of social problem solving
and at worst the use of a tool which is foreign to and
repugnant to oppressed communities whose life styles
are not similarly oriented. Reason is the straight-
jacket into which the liberal forces other peoples.
It is the criterion which ultimately is "unreasonable"
for those whose existences are built on oppression,
rage, rape, and agony - all those qualities to life
that reason does not really touch. The liberal's insistence that words and acts meet the western standards
of reason is his subtle way of controlling the ball
game: reason is his rule which he, as the umpire, en-
forces. Telling the starving to be reasonable, or
those being genocided to reason together is a means of
continuing exploitation. Life, for others than the
comfortable, does not operate on "reasonable" terms.

Because the liberal assumes that man is good and
may be made reasonable, he interprets history as a
series of morally progressive events, and this assumption is also unsubstantiated. It would be more likely
for most of the world's peoples to view history as
either an experience of continued suffering or, at best,
a mixed bag of temporary pleasures and constant pain.
When Aretha Franklin sings that there "Ain't No Way,"

she is describing far more that the trauma of an un-
requited love affair. This "ain't no way" reflects a
more total pessimism about the general relations one's
context provides him. The intensity of the negation in
the song evidences a history of disaster, the despair
of a people which is unrelenting and, if progressive in
any fashion, is progressive in its agony! Long before
Miss Franklin, Nat Turner's companions were called to
meeting by the black spiritual which told them to,

> "Steal away, steal away,
> Steal away to Jesus.
> Steal away, steal away home;
> I hain't got long to stay here."

The point of the spiritual was more political than
theological. Turner's people were being commanded to
steal away from the brutalizing system which had gotten
them in bonds, a system which gave no hope and was
worth dying against through revolution or any means
necessary. One way or another, through life or death,
the slaves "hain't got long to stay here." History was
not encouraging, it did not turn out to be morally progressive; and escape from its conditions were a necessity even if that meant terminating one's own historical
involvement.

The liberal's faith in the historical process is
misleading. History has been kind to the liberal, of
course, through the past four centuries. But, in truth
if history progresses, its progression occurs in sin-
ister as well as in supportive ways. The structures
within history grow more complex; political and social
systems are further bureaucratized; technology devel-
opes into more sophisticated forms; patterns of culture are more intricate; but, the value of the progression is ambiguous. While the white liberal in
America has reaped benefits from this progress, most
other groups have been raped by the forms evolved from

the process. None of this suggests the possibility of
a return to earlier forms or the reality of withdrawal
from the process as is attempted by some hippie communes; rather, most social groups are simply unable
to view these developments as inevitably beneficial.
The liberal's faith in progress dismisses the major
historical events of our era: the current wars, the
decimation of peoples in and outside of America, even
the natural disasters over which man has not established - or has chosen not to establish - his dubious
controls. If history were consistently meaningful for
people, the blues would be meaningless, and so would
drug culture, the reliance on political despotism, and
the imperialists' "defense" arsenals. It is exploitive
to interpret history as inevitably morally progressive;
it dismisses the existences of the masses; it plays
the Darwinian social fiddle while history's peoples
burn.

These liberal assumptions contribute to a further
and most damaging liberal affirmation: the priority of
the individual over the group. It is his exaltation of
the individual at the expense of community which puts
the liberal into direct conflict with groups which seek
power. The white liberal is not worried about particular blacks or chicanos who achieve. He is scared to
hell, however, when he turns on the television and sees
a mass of raised fists and shouts of "power to the
people" or "black power ." The communal implications
horrify him. When the people, meaning the masses of
oppressed, or the blacks as a group attempt power plays,
there is no question of how white the white liberal
really is! The liberal rationalizes his stance by
claiming that interpersonal relations are the basis of
society's functioning and that it is the responsibility
of persons to understand one another, to communicate
more adequately, to treat one another with respect. He
assumes a kind of snowballing effect to all this, i.e.
if I am humane in my immediate relations and others
whom I meet are as well, the society as a whole is in-

fluenced. Liberals such as the late Adlai Stevenson
quote "one candle in the dark" phrases without noting
that the one candle in the dark is usually snuffed out
by important group breezes - or hurricanes. For it is
collectivities which determine how a society is moved,
not individuals, and a failure to identify with such
power groups becomes one's contribution to those self-
interested communities which will determine events.

The liberal himself is able to exploit not because
of his individual power but because of the groups which
he represents. He is able to affirm individual worth,
striving and accomplishment because the bourgeoisie of
which he is a part has already won his inter-community
battles and provided its own with this idealogy of individualism. And since the white liberal isn't black
and isn't poor, he can afford not to commit himself to
the power approaches of those groups and further his
own interests by discouraging individuals who are black
or poor from identification with them.

The liberal's self-interest is most evident when he
promulgates non-violence and pacifism among the black and
poor. And, here, I would differ with the assassinated
black prophet. Had Dr. King used non-violence only as a
temporary tactic, it would have been justified. In
Montgomery, 1956 and after, violence could have been and
was easily repressed with some who were violent (and
non-violent) simply being exterminated by the police.
But to claim non-violence as a consistently relevant
principle is another thing, and it is the white liberals' "thing" most of all. It is convenient for the
liberal to keep groups non-violent, tactically and on
the basis of principle, not because of the moral superiority of the method as Gandhi, King and white liberals
have claimed, but because a violent establishment has so
little to fear when its victims pledge themselves to
peace. They may be easily overcome. The requirements
of social progress, however, may be quite different. In
the Hitler era, former pacifists as well as the generals

who attempted the plot against Hitler recognized that
the question of violence as a principle was beside the
point. The eradication of Hitler was the necessary goal
which justified any relevant actions. In the American
ghettos, more violence will be inevitable before any
type of community control or self-preservation is established. The liberal distrusts the possibilities of
group violence, because such actions challenge his dominance. In typical fashion, the liberal uses the ab-
stract principle or ideal in order to prevent the concrete, threatening event. He tranquilizes the exploited
with an idealogy unrelated to their needs.

Group action, group power, and sometimes group violence are the prerequisites to authentic modifications
in society. In terms of re-ordering a social system,
we are not important because of our individual identi-
fications but because of our group participations. A
society doesn't exist on the basis of its interpersonal
niceties but on the basis of its intergroup struggles.
To counsel the oppressed to strive for individual
merits only is to counsel the continuation of oppression
To advise against the use of force and, in some instances, violence is to advise the acceptance of exploitation. The white liberal does both and in so doing
intensifies his participation in the rape of the powerless and demolishes any credibility he might have had
with the powerless.

It is clear in the 1970's that it is no longer possible to depend upon leadership which conceives of human
nature or selfless, or reason as the vehicle for change,
or history as morally progressive, or the individual of
integrity as the major agent of change. The liberal who
espouses this ideology is not believable. And it is
certain that there is no national hero at present who is
ideologically liberal and about whom large numbers of
Americans are willing to gather. Hubert Humphrey never
had such a following: McGovern, McCarthy, and Muskie
don't now. Had Robert Kennedy lived, his constituency

might have been attracted partly by such an ideology
but only partly. When one talks with white Alabama
truck drivers or steelworkers from Pittsburgh who liked
Kennedy but later voted for George Wallace, one begins
to understand the Robert Kennedy charisma as an appeal
much broader than and, in many cases, in spite of liberal affirmations. In the 1970's, we will experience
the continuing demise of the liberal politician as both
the ideological right and left move from the center.
We will also see much more of a politics making for
strange bedfellows, as evidenced already in the visits
begun by black militants to southern segregationist
governors in an attempt at an unholy alliance against
court desegregation verdicts. But, the rejection of
the liberal exploiter will not necessarily include an
overcoming of liberal assumptions. Indeed, it is my
feeling that most revolutionary groups in the nation
in the 1970's will inadvertently prove they are the
inheritors of the irrelevancies of liberal ideology.

Of course, no political revolution is occurring in
this nation at this time if by "revolution" one means
the successful re-ordering of the socio-economic-
political structures of a society, the replacement of
old structures by new ones. Possibilities for such
replacing are dim. By saying this, I am not also saying that there is no need of revolution, nor am I dis-
missing the tremendous amount of literature being produced by those who encourage revolution. I am claiming, instead, that there is no group within American
society presently which is both able and willing to
effect such events. Twenty-three million blacks have
not yet decided that revolution would not also mean
their total genocide and, as black radicals affirm,
fifty million younger whites are not revolting. The
dialogue which follows the Mark Rudd session in this
volume includes a heated exchange between blacks and
whites who distrust each others' revolutionary motives.
There is some historical evidence for the black charge
that revolutionary white youth have only an occasional

commitment to action which they ultimately outgrow by
taking a wife, raising a family, and moving to
Scarsdale! The burning of a Bank of America branch in
California or even college R.O.T.C. buildings is
still an isolated act. The more usual is marching and
letting the police know that they are "facist pigs,"
events which hardly restructure a society. Further,
the most usual white approach is the interest in "par-
ticipatory democracy" whereby there is a shaving of
beards, a putting on of ties, a general conforming to
the middle American criteria of respectability, and
then some lobbying for peace candidates. This working
within the exploitive system, this piecemeal attempt at
progress is something which even the establishment can
condone. And, unless minor change itself is considered
revolutionary - which I am not willing to admit - these
events must be seen as leaving the system untouched.
They also continue the liberal assumption that individual acts by good persons noticeably increase historical progress.

I am claiming that even those groups which are an
acknowledged nuisance to this society are operating on
exploitive, liberal assumptions. The hippie or street
people are a prime example. In Atlanta, as in most
metropolitan centers in the nation, there is an area of
many square blocks which is largely populated by the
transient young, many of whom are involved with drugs,
and most of whom think their style of existence is
radically different from the larger society's and
thus a challenge to it. But, being an on-again off-
again thorn in the flesh and of occasional nuisance is
hardly a threat to this city's established ways of doing things. While the hippie sub-culture appears to be
creative, the beginning of an alternate style or
counter culture, it is hardly revolutionary. Most
hippies are noticeable by their withdrawal from political confrontation; they have no secure ideology
which might overcome middle America's, and they exist
in their Atlanta streets only by the tolerance of a

city government which rightly knows the absence of a
real threat when it sees it.

Hippies, who supposedly have revived a serious
ethic of community as against liberal culture's individualism, are not so communal as transient. A close
analysis of hippie life reveals that most - although
not all - communes established are unlasting, with a
succession of personnel while they last, and plagued by
serious disagreements concerning the meaning of responsibility for residents. Thus, hippie culture can
hardly be claimed to be the new monasticism, as some
Catholics are saying, not because of the obvious differences in sexual mores but because of the lack of
communal intent. The watchword which really charac-
terizes the hippie movement is "doing one's own thing"
not doing the community's thing. The hippie formation
of communities is not done for the sake of the community itself but in order to secure enough protection for
the continuing of one's own thing. Thus, hippie culture is the drawing out of an exaggerated individualism
with which these largely middle class youths have been
inculcated by liberal culture. The assumption that one
can and should be doing his own thing is a liberal assumption and is anti-revolutionary, for one's own thing
can never be the basis for a re-ordering of power
structures which themselves are highly organized and
efficient groups programmed to easily overcome individual deviance. Successful revolutionary action is
based on doing a group's thing even when this conflicts
with one's own. Hippie culture is proving that nuisance based on liberal assumptions is not of revolutionary value.

The new left organizations such as the Students
for a Democratic Society and Womens' Liberation present
what first appears to be a more consistently anti-lib-
eral posture. The use of Marxist rhetoric, the group
consciousness, the reliance upon foreign revolutionaries for their heroes, and the explicit attempt to

correlate their actions with blacks, Cubans, etc. provides a frightening picture for the white liberal who
assumes that these persons have nothing in common with
him or his ideals. He is correct in the first instance:
the new left is more adamantly opposed to liberal political leaders than to conservatives affirming that conservative exploitation is less dangerous because of its
transparency. In the second instance, however, the
white liberal is partially mistaken, for the new left
is not nearly so divorced from liberal ideals as it
claims. Instead, following the example of Karl Marx,
the new left in the United States today modifies liberal assumptions while continuing them. As Karl Marx
was very much the product of a western, bourgeois society whose interests in materialism he reflected, so
the new American left is the product of a liberal culture whose exploitive assumptions it reflects.

   The new left does not reject the liberal assumption of the goodness of human nature, it simply iden-
tifies this goodness with a certain group. For the
left, the revolutionary cadre is the most perfect expression of man at the time, an expression which other
men could participate in. The new left's uncritical
assessment of self reaches proportions where the revolutionary group is treated messianically, the saving
instrument which - if it keeps the faith - maintains a
purity against which the gates of hell shall not prevail. The revolutionary organization becomes in essence the Hebraic people of God, or the Roman Catholic
Church of the 13th century, or the liberal intellectual
establishment of the latter 19th: goodness unimpaired
by evil is not debated, it is assumed; meaning un-
diluted by non-meaning need not be questioned, for the
revolutionary it is a given. The only possibility of
eroding this character is the acceptance of a non-
revolutionary stance. In this case, it is not a rejection of the goodness of human nature for the group
but a falling from the group which, by definition,
means evil. Thus, for the new left, history may be

played out largely like a western flick: the good guys
against the bad. The liberal assumption of the possibility of human nature being good, however, is not
overcome. It is only modified to pertain to a particular group.

The liberal's overestimate of the value of reason
is only partially corrected by the new left. Ostensibly, the left is not so interested in the rationale
behind revolution as the creation of power to make for
revolution. The new left supposedly rejects the liberal claim that social progress can be built around
reasonable men. However, the experience of a new left
meeting reveals their very western need for argumenta-
tion, documentation, reasoning out the need of revolution, reasoning out the methods of revolting, etc.
In fact, the new left is spending most of its energy
on conversion through rationales. For every bank
burned, for every college occupied, the left expends
hours showing the uninitiated the reasonableness of
revolution. While these groups do see the naivete in
the liberals' expectations from reason, they depend
upon reason as their method of creating revolutionary
community. In the new left, acts of power have not
displaced the western man's implicit faith in reason;
in practice if not in ideology these revolutionaries
are rationally oriented.

Most important, the new left accepts a liberal
view of history as a process in which there is moral
progression. If anything, the new left is more subservient to utopian ideals than liberalism. For the
revolutionary, there is a religiosity about this hoped
for, expected event: a society without oppression, a
kingdom of God on earth, is coming through the revolution. The left takes the possibility of classless-
ness too seriously believing that social phenomena can
be structured to each one's needs, and the revolution
and its suffering become worthwhile because of this end
which is to be effected. Moral ambiguities of all

historical development are beside the point for the
radical young, for man through revolution may expect to
overcome present ambiguities, the defeat of future exploiters, the creation of adequate societies. The new
left believes it owes these concepts to Marx but, again
Marx was indebted to western, bourgeois idealism and in
this case the Hegel and the 19th century German ideal-
ists whom he materialized. The acceptance of inevitable moral progress through revolution differs only in
its method from the liberal assumption that history is
perfectible. For the new left, it is the action of the
group which creates the great society, for the liberal
it is the good-natured individual. The two approaches
share a mutual unreality about the negativities of
future history.

    The question of revolution in America will not be
determined by protesting whites who are unable to
resist liberal assumptions and who, thus far, have been
unable to provide a broad proletarian base. Instead,
it is the black community which represents the potential revolutionary force within this nation. This is
implicitly recognized by the new left whose own development has followed the successes of the black rights
movements. In fact, the new left could create itself
only after Montgomery in 1956, the Selma march, and
summers in Mississippi. The organizational structures
of the old left, such as the American Communist Party,
have never been attractive to young radicals in the
1960's, and the youth argue that those traditional
groups are ideologically too rigid and function too
bureaucratically. In spite of Marxist verbiage, the
new left is noteworthy in its continued dependence upon
what blacks are saying and doing. The new left's heroes
are either black or foreign; they almost never come
from the white American community. The Students for a
Democratic Society and Women's Liberation make extra-
ordinary attempts to ally themselves with black movements, particularly the Black Panther Party and, although this is rationalized in terms of the black's

best interests, these groups are aware that the black
man is the answer to the revolutionary question and
other revolutionaries must not be far out of line with
the demands of black leadership. All of this estab-
lishes an ironic situation, for black radicals are dis-
dainful of white activists, refuse to be used by them,
and assume quite correctly that they are only partially
dependable followers. And, so leadership roles are
quite reversed among the young radicals: in liberal
America it was the blacks who needed the whites; in
the third American revolution, it will be the whites who
need the blacks.

The black community is the only major group in this
country which can reject the erroneous assumptions of
liberalism since it alone has never accepted those assumptions. In spite of the idealism whites have clung
to about all of us being "brothers under the skin," the
black man in America has successfully maintained his
otherness, his difference. White liberals have not
westernized him, liberalized him, made him rational
according to European philosophical standards or, quite
bluntly, made him behave! The black ethics of deception and rejection have worked so that the black community continues as the counter community in this society. There is, of course, a portion of that community
which acquiesces, the so-called black bourgeoisie, but
its attempts to out-honkify even the white middle class
are not representative. Further, the renaissance of
interest in black culture is certainly eliminating the
black bourgeoisie as a criterion and is becoming the
important vehicle for a re-alliance between the masses
of the ghettoized and the black intellectuals.

One needs to live within the black areas of large
cities to have his liberal ideals about the oneness of
all peoples totally shattered; teaching in black
schools or working with blacks on jobs is not enough.
It takes one's neighbors, one's constant acquaintances
to prove the differences between blacks and whites which,

more than likely, they are glad to do! One gets an
inkling of the black distinctiveness if he takes
seriously the poetry of LeRoi Jones, or the sophisticated street mythologies of Robert DeCoy in THE
NIGGER BIBLE, or the words of the black prince, Malcolm
X. It is this difference, not forced but quite natural,
which is happening and which - in spite of liberal
ideology and the presence of a black bourgeoisie - has
always happened. The blacks are the other in America,
the counter people, the group which has always been
foreign in someone else's land. The recurring historical attempts at liberation and, particularly, the continued interest in black nationalism are evidences of
the black's own awareness of his foreignness. Whites
don't realise it, but the Muslims are but a latter-day
version of a nationalistic intent which has been usual
not unusual in the black community, and which was expressed by Marcus Garvey in the 1920's plus a number of
black churchmen who began what they hoped would be now
black nations both in America and Africa.

The otherness of the black involves the clearest
challenge to the exploitation and ideology of the white
liberal. Black tradition encourages an approach to
reality which is wholly outside the liberal's historical categories and which depends instead on an affinity
with nature, something the liberal has not been too
interested in. The black needs no definite historical
scheme, no secure ideology by western standards, no
rationalized process on which he must base his action.
He is freer, unbound by theories which must be kept,
as his African orientations give him a kind of assumed
indentification with the natural he meets. The only
group of the new left which comes close to this appreciation. of and response to nature as the basic category
of reality is the Yippies. Their attempts to "mess-up"
the establishment's mind by doing the natural, however,
is a fabulous fake! It is doing of what is unnatural
even to them in order to disturb what is historically
normal to others. Blacks don't have to engage in what
is not natural to them in order to naturally disturb

the oppressor. Their heritage outside of western standards of reason, goodness, progress is a given which is
not simulated. This is why the ghetto man remains
quite unbelievable to the white liberal after 350 years
of attempted acculturation. It is why the total group
keeps its identity far beyond distinctions of color
after 350 years of rape which often extended to genocide. It is why the black talks about "doing his own
thing" and means doing his whole group's thing as opposed to the white thing. Thus, the blacks' otherness
is a distinctively communal otherness which continues
the interest in community known in African tribalism,
and it has proven to be maintainable.

Communal rage, suffering and secure identification,
however, do not necessarily make for revolution. As
Leon Trotsky claimed, "What distinguishes a revolutionary in his willingness to die." And while the black
community is the potential proletariate, the question
of its willingness to die more than it already has is
not yet answered. Whites must remember that blacks
treat experience with the kind of dialectical integrity
which gives them a perspective on reality not always
shared by white revolutionaries. The black is much
more consistent in affirming the ambiguities of good
and bad in persons and their acts and, thus, is quite
suspicious of revolutionary idealism and those who
espouse it. Blacks are not likely to promote their
own extermination and especially on behalf of non-
blacks. They have been too close to the possibility
in this country too many times before and are unwilling
to risk the unriskable. Blacks are acutely aware of
the fact that they are not the ones who can go home to
Scarsdale, and they continue their disdain for those
who can. White interpreters of black leaders ordinarily suggest attitudes which don't exist. For example,
Marxist authors like to claim that Malcolm repudiated
his former suspicions of whites and was aligning himself with the largely white socialist movements in the
world. This was not the case. Malcolm's trips abroad
did introduce him to the possibilities of whites also
being revolutionaries, particularly in Algeria, but he

never made an accommodation with the kinds of occasional
revolutionaries we find in this country. His thing
continued to be a black thing undetermined by Marxists
or the new left. And, young blacks following him today
insist upon answering their own revolutionary questions
apart from the biases of the radical whites.

        In the 1970's, then, revolutionary attempts in
America will be fumbling exercises not because they a
are not needed but because those most victimized, most
raped, have not determined their methods of partici-
patiog in the gaining of power. The white liberal has
dug his own political grave. He is no longer the hero,
and his ideological assumptions have been proven exploitive. The dismissal of the liberal exploiter,
however, does not guarantee the successful entree of
revolutionary action. Arendt and other interpreters of
the twentieth century insist that revolution is one of
the two central political issues of our time. But one
must also insist that men do not easily revolt. Instead, most of mankind endures the rape of its communities for interminable lengths of time, and there is a
clear reason for this: their communities are relatively powerless. Therefore, the question of the liberal
exploiter and his future is answerable; the question
of revolution in this country is not. It will be
answered, however, by those groups of potential such
as the blacks who will interpret their own present
desperations, assess their own possibilities of power,
and accomplish their own destinies.